Quitting Was Not An Option

A Journey of Perseverance and Resilience

Dr. John E. Gray

Copyright © 2019 John E. Gray, Ed.D

All rights reserved.

ISBN-13: 978-1-5136-4639-8

DEDICATION

I dedicate this book to my mother, whose spirit I feel every day. I also dedicate this book to my father, who I grew to understand better as I became a husband and father. Lastly, I dedicate this book to my wife, Angie, who met a man with a fractured spirit and helped me become a better version of myself.

Table of Contents

ACKNOWLEDGMENTS

I want to acknowledge everyone who played a part in my journey. Whether the experience was good or bad, the learning experience was an invaluable part of my growth as a man, father and husband.

1976

Every journey to success has pivotal moments. If you ask anyone who has achieved any measure of success they can point clearly to those defining moments that shaped who they would eventually become. Mind you, this is not the moment they became successful, but it was in these moments that something sparked from within. Even though they may, or may not, have realized it at that time, these moments were when things got set in motion.

My first moment coincides with the title of this chapter – 1976. This was the year my life would change forever. I was the youngest of nine children, indeed, I was my mother's baby. I was only seven years old when my mother, who was fighting breast cancer at the time, gathered all her children together and told us she was going to die. I cannot remember all the details from that day, but I do remember that we did not believe it. I also recall us making jokes about what we each wanted in the house, and calling dibs on certain things. There was no reason to think this would be different from any of the previous times. Mom had been sick before, but she always came home.

As far back as I could remember, there had been a family friend who would stop by and check on us, but we were usually left by ourselves. My mother smoked, and I remember hearing that she was going, back and forth, to the hospital because of the cigarettes. This made one of her returns home puzzling to me. One day, my mother returned home from the hospital after one of her visits and went straight to the neighborhood bar where she worked occasionally. It was not unusual for us kids to tag along. The bar was our daycare on many occasions. To me, it was a normal thing. When she got to the bar, the whole place erupted into cheers. Everybody started hugging my mother. One person gave her a drink, and another, gave her a cigarette. It was only after years of reflection that it dawned on me how asinine that was. Why in the world would you give someone who just came out of the hospital a drink and a cigarette? Back in the early 1970s, there was not a whole lot of knowledge about cancer. Today, so many breakthroughs either save or extend the lives of those with cancer. However, if you were poor back then, there was every likelihood that you would be in the dark about this horrible disease. Maybe mother's friends thought she had beat it and they were celebrating. It's hard for me to rationalize. All I know is that, I felt just like them. I could not fathom life without my mother. No matter what she told us whenever she gathered us together; there was no way she was going to leave us forever. In my seven-year-old mind, that wasn't possible. She could not leave us, and she, definitely, would not leave her baby!

Growing up, we never had a lot, but what I do know, was that my mother loved us. As a single mother in the 1970s, holding it down by herself, we struggled and struggled, a lot. My brothers, sisters, and I had different fathers, and as far as I can recall, none of them was ever around for any consistent amount of time. They would make appearances, but as far as being present providers, that was not the case at all. I often tell people that my family was "PO," because we could not even afford the "OR." We spent days in the dark when the light were cut off. We had to use the stove to heat the house and dry our clothes. We also placed our clothes on the radiator to dry them. I had no idea what a washing machine looked like. We did not have money to go to the laundromat, so we hand-washed our clothes in the sink. I also vividly remember washing up in the large basin sink in the kitchen. We went hungry a lot. To this day, I do not eat onion soup, neither do I have any love for onions, because we, oftentimes, only had cans of onion soup in the cabinet.

Our family had to get creative. My brothers, sisters, and I would make up different kinds of food. We would make sugar sandwiches.

We did this by putting sugar in the middle of a piece of bread, fold it up, and that was the sandwich! We would make ketchup and mustard sandwiches the same way we made the sugar sandwiches. We went without the necessities a lot, and wore the same clothes to schools often. I even remember the roaches in our cereal boxes. And we better not had thrown away that cereal either! My mother would have whipped our behinds if we wasted good cereal over a few roaches. We would pluck the roaches off the table, mix some water with powdered milk, and go about our business. To many in this present day, the thought of eating cereal that had roaches crawling around in it sounds disgusting and unhygienic. To that I will say this: If you are hungry enough you will be surprised at what you will eat. Shame goes out the window when hunger sets in.

I also remember that I was a huge fan of Jackson 5, and I remember when they made a song about a rat named Ben. Such a nice song, but when I was much younger, the last thing I wanted to see or sing about was a rat. This was because of a terrifying incident I had involving a rat. One night while I was asleep, I felt something crawling on my leg. I woke up and saw a huge rat on me! I screamed and screamed. My mother came in with one of those heavy old-school mops and killed the rat. From that point on, there would be no singing of love songs to rats for me, no matter how much I loved the Jackson 5!

I also recall a time when I really wanted to join our neighborhood basketball team. The sneakers that I had was so worn-down, that the soles were almost gone. I ran home to my mother and told her I really wanted to play basketball, but I needed some new sneakers. My mother said to me, "We don't have money for sneakers, so you can't play basketball." I was crushed. I really wanted to play, and the other kids teased me unmercifully. Looking back and thinking about this, it's amazing that even though we were all in the ghetto and poor, kids still found a way to pick out something about another person and tease them about it. I was teased a lot in school, especially about my hair. My mother was in the hospital a lot, and it was up to my older siblings to make sure we got to school. Let's just say, there was not a whole lot of attention paid to the details of grooming. I was called "dirty" and "nappy-head" a whole lot. I would then respond by lashing out in anger and it usually ended up in a fight. All because we were poor and my mother was sick. A part of me wanted to play basketball just to show those other kids I could be as good as they were, but my mother was only being honest with me. We did not have the money for sneakers, no matter how bad I wanted them. That was just another example of the many times that we did not have what we needed or wanted. Another incident I clearly remember was when I brought a friend of mine from school to the bar where my mother was working. I asked her if my friend could come to our house for dinner. My mother said, "Hell no. I barely have enough for y'all. I can't feed somebody else's child." As I mentioned earlier, the struggle was very real.

Although we went without a lot of what we wanted or needed, one thing we did have in our home, and in abundance, was love. I remember when our house caught fire, my mother tried to run into the burning house because she thought I was still in there. She would not stop until somebody brought me to her. As I said, my mother loved us. I also remember an incident in school, when my mother came to her baby's defense against a teacher. My mother was a teacher's aide in the school I attended. Even though she was right there in my school, I still found a way to act up in school on occasion. Kids will be kids no matter what, so I acted as a typical child would. On this day, my teacher made a comment about slapping some sense into me, and I ran to my mother to tell her. My mother went right to that class and told the teacher off! I loved it! She would not tolerate anybody attempting to put their hands on any of her children. If anybody was going to lay hands on her kids, it was going to be her and nobody else! So, when she told us she was going away and never coming back, I just knew she would not leave us. She could not. She loved us too much to leave us.

One day in the summer of 1976, my mother went to the hospital again. We waited for her to come home but she did not. We thought things would be normal when she came back home as she always did. But things would never be the same again. The next day, a brown car came to our house. Being seven years old, I was wondering why the car had the sun on the side of the door. I found out later that it was not the sun, but the seal of the state of New Jersey. The car came to take us to foster homes. One by one, my brothers, sisters, and I would be taken into a stranger's house. That was the last time myself, or my brothers and sisters, would ever spend the night together as a family. No more Christmas days together. No more Thanksgivings together. No more birthdays together. From that moment on, my family was splintered, and would never be whole again. We were now the responsibility of the State of New Jersey. From that moment until I turned 18, I was a ward of the state.

That was the moment I knew my mother was not lying to us when she told us she was dying. Normally, when my mother got sick and went to the hospital, we would stay at the house. Neighbors and friends then checked on us at various times. This time was different. There would be no neighborhood check-ins. My mother had a sense of her own mortality. She had struggled with her health for so long. I even remembered when they had to remove her breasts. My mother knew the end was drawing near for her. She knew she would not see her 40th birthday, which was only about three months away. She was preparing us for the reality of her death. Imagine this through the lens of a seven-year-old. Imagine trying to process this, as everything you knew as normal was changing. Imagine trying to cope with this in a stranger's house. This was my new reality, and this was one of those moments that would shape me.

A woman named Mrs. Little took in my brother Larry, my sister Wanda, and me. I don't remember much about that time, but I do remember the feeling of sadness, loneliness, and hurt. All I wanted was my mother. I did not understand why we had to be in this person's house when my mother was still coming home from the hospital. I did not understand why I could not be with the rest of my brothers and sisters. And most of all, I could not understand why Mrs. Little was so mean and why her kids did not like us. Her children would do mischievous stuff around the house and tell us point blank that they were going to tell their mother we did it! I was always a mischievous child myself, and usually had no problem getting into trouble on my own.

I remember, very clearly, one incident where my siblings and I decided we wanted to play on the phone. So, we went to a public phone booth and called the operator. When the operator answered, we would curse them out and hang up the phone. We did this at least ten times. When we got home, my mother gave us all a beating. I found out later that my older sister Debbie had told on us. My mother lost it! She could not imagine her kids doing something so wrong, and she really went after my brothers and sisters for dragging me along. What she didn't know was that I was all in. Nobody made me do anything, I volunteered! I also remember one other very mischievous moment I had (I had a whole lot of them). My mother used to love Al Green! She would play Al Green all day, all night. Love and Happiness. I'm So Tired of Being Alone. And her all-time favorite; For the Good Times. But there was one small problem. I didn't like Al Green and I was tired of hearing Al Green. I was even tired of looking at the album cover, the one with him in the big white chair smiling. One day, I noticed someone had left some records on the windowsill, and the sun ruined the records. In my five-year-old head, I plotted to put the Al Green album on the windowsill, so it could get ruined like the other records did. I did it and my plan worked! The album was ruined and there would be no more Al Green! When my mother saw her favorite album all messed up, she concluded my brothers and sisters did it, and handed out the whippings. I didn't get a beating, because of course, her little baby wouldn't do anything like that. I felt bad for my brothers and sisters, but I didn't confess. It was only when we were all grown that I fessed up and told them. As I said, I could earn my own beatings. That's why I couldn't stand getting the beatings for stuff the other kids did, and I hated them more and more. All I could think about in my head was, "Wait until my mother gets home. She's gonna beat y'all up!" I couldn't wait for my mother to come home and do to that woman what she did to that teacher. She would protect me and make sure nobody hurt me again. I would never see that confrontation.

True to her word, my mother passed away on August 16, 1976. I did get one more chance to see her before she died, and she made me promise to be good. I promised my mother I would be good, and I never saw her again after that. What I remember mostly is that my mother did not look sickly even unto death. She looked like she did in previous times when she got up, out of that hospital bed, and came home to us. As I left the hospital, I had no idea that would be the last time I saw her. In my mind, she would be home soon. By this time, our grandparents in South Jersey had taken us in. They lived in Lawnside, and I hated living there. I used to wake up every morning crying because I hated it so much. I wanted to go back to Newark so badly! I wanted to see my father, my aunts, and my cousins.

It was obvious that my grandmother did not want us there. My grandfather, who was actually my step-grandfather, was different. I thought my grandmother was the meanest person on earth, but he was not mean to us at all. In retrospect, he did the very best he could, given the way the situation unfolded. He was enjoying his home, just he and his wife. All of a sudden, here comes some kids he did not count on. He used to talk to us a lot about life, and although I did not appreciate it then, I learned to appreciate it when I became a grown married man with children of my own. He was very fair to us, but he usually let my grandmother handle all things pertaining to us. Except for one moment that I will never forget.

That day, the phone rang. My grandmother and grandfather ran out of the house without saying a word. We thought nothing of it, and went outside to play. A short while later, we were in the backyard still playing, then I heard a lot of screaming and crying. My grandfather came outside, gathered me, my brother Larry, and my sisters Wanda and Rosie together. Then, he told us our mother had died. Just like that. Your mother died. Just three words, that changed my life forever. Your mother died. As the years went by, I was especially angry about two things: One, my grandmother did not even take it upon herself to tell us; and two, why in the world would you tell four little kids their mother has passed away in only three words? Upon hearing this devastating news from my grandfather, my brother, sisters, and I went inside to cry with everyone else. What happened next was one of those defining moments. My grandmother told us kids to "sit down and shut up all that damn crying." I looked at her like she was crazy! I thought to myself, "What do you mean, stop all that damn crying?" Our mother just died, and we can't cry? You hate us so much that you won't even allow us to cry?

I watched in disbelief as all the adults in the room screamed and cried over my mother, but we were told to shut up. There were people in the house that I did not even know, and they were crying. Yet, we were told to shut up. I looked at my brother Larry and my sister Wanda, and they had this blank look on their faces. They were there, but they were not there. I asked my sister why grandmom had told us to stop crying, but she ignored me. Looking back on that moment, I don't even think she heard me. Something happened to all of Catherine's kids on that day, and time has still not healed all of the wounds. Whoever said that time heals all wounds, lied. Time may sooth most of the hurt, but some wounds still fester. We were forced to grow up quickly that day. That would be the last time we had someone to fully protect us. We were forced to stuff our pain deep down and pretend to be normal. This was one of those moments that shaped who I would become. I call this a seminal moment, because I learned at an early stage, that in order to function I had to push past my pain.

What I did not know, at that time, was my grandmother, in her misguided way, blamed my mother's passing on us, the children. What I now realize is that, she was hurting over the loss of her only child. My grandmother never talked to us about our mother. Having lost my mother at such an early age, I truly believe it would have helped my healing process if I could have talked about her more. Or if I could have had someone guide me through the entire ordeal. I never understood why my grandmother resented us so much. I could never have imagined the depths of her grief or anger at me and my siblings over my mother's death. To add insult to our grief, she even refused to acknowledge the children on my mother's headstone. Whenever I visit my mother's gravesite, the stone simply reads: Catherine L. Gray 1936-1976. There is only one other word inscribed on the headstone – daughter. I visit my mother's gravesite often, and it is still painful to see just that word "daughter" inscribed on the headstone.

There have been many times where I said I would replace it

entirely. But I have still not done so. A part of me wants to keep it that way as a reminder of sorts. I also think I keep it there as proof of the depths of my journey. There are a whole lot of people who may not believe someone's grandmother would be capable of doing such a thing. I have rarely shared this with anyone, with the exception of a rare few. The few people who I have shared a moment with, at my mother's gravesite, were taken aback at the fact that her children were not even acknowledged. It is almost as though we never existed. In many ways, I was made to feel like I did not exist, and I harbored so much resentment because of it. I felt like the moment my mother died, I ceased to be important to anyone. I felt alone in a crowded world. I felt like I had to fend for myself emotionally. For better or for worse, I had to deal with my mother's loss on my own.

What I find ironic to this day is that while my grandmother sought to exclude us by not placing the word "mother" on the headstone; she currently has no identifying headstone at her gravesite, and she is buried right next to my mother. When my grandfather remarried, shortly after my grandmother died, he did not finish paying for her grave marker. The down payment he put down on my grandmother's headstone was his final act of matrimony. I have talked about this several times with my siblings. At any given moment, any one of us, or each of us as a collective, could have bought a headstone and placed it at my grandmother's grave. My brother Larry had the best relationship with my grandmother. He stayed with her until she passed away. He told me, years later, that he came to understand her better and that she did have some regrets as time passed by. Yet, he has not purchased a headstone for her, either. Some may say to me that I should be more conscientious, and out of respect, buy a headstone for her. However, if I am honest, I cannot bring myself to do it. I cannot even bring myself to have a graveside chat with her whenever I visit my mother's grave. I cannot recall one time when I said, "Hi Grandmom." There was something within me that got damaged to the core, and I have spent most of my life trying to move past that damage and hurt. As a Christian, I know what forgiveness entails. However, if I can be transparent, I am still struggling, to this day, with processing the rejection, abuse, and isolation I encountered.

I was only a baby when I lost my family, yet I was left to navigate a dark forest by myself.

As time passes, many memories get lost. What I have learned is what many psychologists have professed in their research. People do two things with a traumatic experience. They either shove it into the far regions of their psyche, where it lies dormant until something awakens it. On the other hand, they develop a sort of video memory, where the incident is as indelible as the day it occurred, and it keeps playing back repeatedly. The memory of my mother's funeral falls with the latter. I cannot tell you most of the details, but there are two that are clear-lit and will never forget. The first was the fact that my father was not there. Losing my mother was hard enough, but not having my father around to help me deal with it, made it harder. My grandmother gave us no opportunity to mourn, so, I had no idea how to process this in my seven-year-old mind. I hoped beyond hope that my father, at some point, would step in and help me make sense of this nightmare. On one hand, it did not seem real, yet on the other, it felt all too real. I remember looking around during the funeral and watching the door, hoping to see him come in, but he never did.

The second thing that I remember, and will never forget, is how my mother looked and felt. My mother was wearing a yellow dress and I remember that she looked so sad. She had a frown on her face. Because the immediate family is usually on the first row at funerals, we had a clear view of the casket. The casket remained open the whole time, and I wanted to look away, but I could not. I just kept thinking to myself how sad she looked! Years later, when my brother and I were grown men with families of our own, we talked about mommy's funeral for the first time. Without hesitation, we both brought up how sad she looked. As a child, I thought she was sad because she was no longer with us. I internalized that look of sadness on her face and it has remained with me ever since. I also will never forget how she felt. As I was escorted to the casket to see her, I grabbed her hand, and immediately pulled my hand back. That did not feel like my mother's hand! Her hand was cold and hard, no warmth at all. I automatically connected death with the feeling of her hand, and it made me so afraid. For years after that, I harbored a fear of dying, because of what I saw and felt at my mother's funeral.

As I stood by her casket, I began to cry. I am thankful, at least, that my grandmother gave me this moment to cry. Looking back now, I realize people would have thought she was crazy if she told me to stop crying at my own mother's funeral. It was at that moment I felt totally lost. I was hoping that she would just wake up. What seven-year-old can rationalize the death of a parent? When I was told that my mother died, I could not perceive it, and thought that she would walk back through the door. At the funeral, I somehow thought she would wake up from this sad sleep. Even when they closed the casket, I did not grasp the finality of her death. As long as I could see the casket and knowing that she was still in there, I still held out hope that she would get up again.

I was not prepared for what came next. What occurred was one of those video moments featuring years of nightmares for me. We drove to the Sunset Memorial Cemetery in Pennsauken, NJ. As we got out of the cars, I saw the family walking towards a large hole dug in the ground. I had no idea what was going on because nobody told us about the process, nor did they explain what was about to happen. As I watched with curiosity, I saw them place the casket next to this hole. After a short while, they gave me a flower and told me to put it on the casket. I still did not understand what was happening. Then, they began to lower the casket into the ground! I could not believe they were putting my mother into that hole in the ground! I grabbed my sister and screamed, "Why are they putting mommy down there?" My sister Rosie did not answer me. She could not take her eyes off the hole in the ground. I remember the look on the faces of my brothers and sisters. They were in shock. Up to that point, we had not experienced death. We had never attended a funeral. Nobody in our family, to my recollection, had died. We had no prior experience to draw on concerning what was happening to us. What made things worse was when we had to leave. After the flowers were placed on mommy's casket, everybody started to go back to the cars. I recall being so horrified! I thought to myself, "Why are they leaving her there by herself?" All I could think about in my seven-year-old head was how lonely my mother was going to be in the ground.

The gravediggers did not even wait for us to leave completely before they started filling in the hole. As we began to drive away, I looked back and they were working on filling the grave hole. On that day, my soul became numb, and life would never be normal again. To this day, I wish one of the adults would have sat the children down, and at least, tried to explain death to us. I wish they had attempted to explain the funeral process to us. Seeing my mother's casket lowered into the ground was the imprinting of the finality of death for me. She was not getting back up. I would never see her again.

As I said at the beginning of this chapter, everything changed in 1976. My seven-year-old world was shattered. My grief became anger. On the outside, I may have looked like a normal seven-year-old, but I was hurting to my core. And I had no one to help me understand what was happening to me, or help me feel better.

Penn Station

My next defining moment occurred when I was thirteen years old. Up to this point, I had been in and out of foster homes, and ended up living with my grandmother who, often, actually told us that we killed our mother. She would use the phrase, "You kids drove your mother to her grave." I was always in a state of hurt and anger. To make matters worse, I had to go to a new school three weeks after losing my mother. And the first assignment my teacher gave, was to write about what I did that summer!

I did not make a good impression at my new school because I refused to do the assignment. The teacher blurted out to the class, "I see we have a new hard-head student." What she did not know was that I could not bring myself to write about losing my mother and having my world torn apart. How do I share that with a strange teacher in a strange school in front of a strange class?

In hindsight, I never did fit in during those next few years in school. Kids can be cruel and adults can be worse. I got into so many fights because the kids wanted to remind "the new kid" that his mom was dead. Teachers took my demeanor as disobedience and arrogance, when I was only guarding myself against hurt and ridicule. I was losing faith in adults because I felt like I had no one who loved me. I was shuffling between an unloving home life and an uncaring school life. I had one teacher actually call me a stupid little boy, because I did not know an answer to a question. To this day, I can hear the words "stupid little boy" ringing in my years. I carried those words with me through high school, college, and across the stage when I received my doctorate degree. In a strange way, I thank her because I used her slight to fuel me to excel. I even got the chance to tell her as much when I met her again at a teacher's convention. I re-introduced myself to her and she barely recognized me. I condescendingly said, "I'm the stupid little boy from your eighth grade class." As she searched for words, I told her it was okay because I used it to my advantage. She asked what I was doing at the conference, I showed her my convention badge, and said, "I'm here for the same reason you are. I am a teacher."

I must admit, that moment felt good. Teachers called me stupid, I was left back in eighth grade and had to go to summer school so I could get promoted. I had an overall miserable experience in school. Yet, I was able to become a teacher and never do to children what was done to me. When I became a teacher, I swore I would never break the spirit of a child. I would never make them feel less than. I would be considerate of the things that may be going on in their homes. In addition, I have never, in my ten years as a classroom teacher, given the assignment "What did you do over the summer?"

Nevertheless, I digress. During this time in my life, my home life was as bad as my school life. I was dealing with a grandmother who I felt could not stand the sight of me. Maybe I reminded her of my father, but I swear, she could not stand me. I recently had a conversation with my older sister Rosie and she said the same thing. She said she could not understand why grandmom treated me the way she did. She could not understand why she hated me so much. Rosie said, "I don't know why she treated you the way she did but I used to feel so sorry for you." I recall a time when I got in trouble for calling my oldest sister a dirty dog. My sister Debbie yelled out what I called her to my grandmother. On hearing this, my grandmother called me to her room. I fully expected to get in trouble and be on punishment, but what I was not expecting was to be met with a shoe being hurled at my face, busting my nose in the process. I have told this story many times over the years, and have, on occasion, even laughed about it. But here is what I wonder; either my grandmother had such a great aim that she hit me in my nose, or she did not really care where the shoe hit me. Mind you, this was no small lightweight shoe. Rather, one of those old-school grandma shoes with the thick heel. What if that was my eye instead of my nose? Knowing my grandmother as I did, I do not think she really cared if it was my eye or my nose. Not only did she hit me in the face with the shoe, she yelled at me because blood was getting all over her bedroom floor! I bled so much that you would have thought I should have been rushed to a hospital. Instead, I was yelled at, and told to go to the bathroom and clean myself up.

I was a kid who managed to get in trouble a lot. A big part of that was due to my issues with authority. After my mother passed, I would think to myself, "You're not my mother and I don't have to listen to you." I felt that way towards pretty much everybody, so I was always in trouble. What I, often, remember is how my grandmother would punish me. I felt like she beat me with bad intentions. I could feel the hate with each stroke of the belt. It always felt like I got a little extra when it came to my whippings. My brother Larry would get beatings, often because of me, but mine felt harsher. I concluded in my mind that my grandmother hated me, and that is why I ran away from home several times, and was always in trouble. My hurt and frustration had transformed itself into anger and resentment.

I was resentful that I had to live with a grandmother who would often tell us we did not have to live in her house and could leave whenever we were ready to. Oftentimes, I reflect back on those times, and try to recollect any memories that involved my grandmother saying something good to, or about, me. I come up empty after each reflection. After a while, I began to think that something was wrong with me. I began to internalize all the negativity that was thrown at me. I was being ridiculed at home and at school. I had nowhere to turn to, for affirmation and encouragement. I always felt like I had to fight to keep some sense of sanity and dignity. The experience made me bitter and angry. I never heard the words, "I love you" while I was growing up. How can anyone expect a child to grow up and be able to express love, when they never had love modeled for them?

I think my capacity to love came from a God-given place and from holding on to those glimmers of love I received from my mother while she was alive. Now that I think about it, I never heard the words "I love you" from anybody until the day I decided to leave my grandmother's house when I was thirteen years old. The words did not come from my grandmother; they came from my Brother Larry. I will go further into those details in a moment.

While I was dealing with the blows life brought, I carried an idealistic thought in my head. From the moment I lost my mother, I had the feeling that my father would step in and save the day. In this case, the idealized was much better than the realized. I would, on occasion, talk to my father on the phone. Because I did not want my grandmother to know I was calling him, I would go to a phone booth and place a collect call. I knew my grandmother hated my father, but I never knew why. As a child, a part of me hated her because she hated him.

I vividly remember one incident where my grandmother was filling out my free lunch application for school. She gave it to me to take back to school. On the application, one section asked for the parents' names. Next to mother, my grandmother wrote the word deceased. Next to father, she wrote the word unknown. I took the form back to my grandmother and said innocently, "I know who my father is." Without saying a word, my grandmother slapped me in my face and busted my lip. She angrily said, "Just take the damn paper back to school!"

In my thirteen-year-old mind, that was the last straw. I made a decision; I would not take it anymore. I could not and would not stay in her house any longer. I would take her up on her offer and leave. I could not stand to hear how awful we were and how we drove our mother to her death. I was tired of being emotionally and physically abused. Most of all, I was tired of not being loved. Since my mother died, I felt there was nobody who protected me. I was constantly at the mercy of the ridicule and scorn of others. I felt like I had no shepherd to protect me from the wolves.

Moreover, if the shepherd is absent or negligent, the wolves will find their way in. When I was twelve, the wolf came through the door in the guise of a relative. She was not a blood relative, but all my life I called her Aunt Debbie. She was the "cool aunt," and I remember her as someone who was the life of the party. My grandfather loved music, and there was usually a get-together on the weekends at the house. My aunt loved to dance, and she usually made me dance with her. She used to tell me that she was getting me ready for my dates with my future girlfriends. I thought nothing of it because she was my aunt. Things began to get strange when she asked me if I had ever slow-danced with a girl before. I said no, because I was twelve and that wasn't even something I was thinking about. She then told me that after everyone went upstairs she would teach me how. I guess my grandparents did not think anything of it. Aunt Debbie used to say, "I will keep an eye on them for y'all." So, when the rest of the adults went upstairs, she taught me how to slow-dance with a woman. It felt weird, but I initially took it as getting an education of sorts.

I thought she was looking out for me and helping me to not be shy when I did get around girls eventually, and had to dance with them. Those slow dances became sort of a ritual when she came over for a visit. In a boyish sort of way, I thought it was kind of cool. It made me feel more grown up. Then, things took a turn that would change everything. As usual, it started with some cruel thing said by my grandmother. She and my aunt were having a conversation, and somehow, I became the subject. My grandmother made the remark, "John probably doesn't like girls. He's probably gonna be a faggot." They were laughing hysterically and it hurt beyond words! How in the world could that even come out of my grandmother's mouth? This happened to be the catalyst for the molestation that would follow. After my grandmother made that comment, my aunt whispered to me, "I'm gonna find out." Then, she winked at me and walked away.

Later that night, my aunt told my brother Larry to watch the door to the upstairs bedroom and she told me to come upstairs. On that day, my thirty-three-year-old aunt molested her twelve-year-old nephew. She took my virginity and my innocence. I will never forget what she asked me. She asked, "How do you like your women, on top?" Now that I am older, I fully see the nonsensical and predatory nature of that question. I was twelve! How in the hell was I supposed to know how I liked women sexually? My days of seeing life through the lens of a child were gone. How do you continue to be a child when you are placed in such a situation? She then added insult to injury by telling me, "Your mother would have wanted me to take care of you." While I now know that what she used was manipulation; to a twelve-year-old who felt like nobody cared about him, it might sound like a sensible

17

statement. She made it seem like she was keeping a promise to my mother while doing me a favor at the same time. Somewhere deep in my core, I knew this was wrong, but who was I going to tell? I had no one to share what I was going through because, frankly, I did not trust adults. These encounters with Aunt Debbie continued until I was seventeen years old. One thing I will never forget was the look on my Uncle Eddie's face. Uncle Eddie was her husband. I told my brother, "Larry, he has to know what happened. I can tell by his look."

My grandfather knew too. I could tell by the look on his face whenever he left us downstairs in the basement listening to music. But he never said a word. Nobody did. I remember telling my brother Poncho about this several years later. He is eight years older than I am. He pretty much congratulated me and wanted details. Nobody looked at it as molestation because I was a boy and she was a woman, but that is exactly what it was. Her predation made future relationships difficult for me. I had a hard time relating to women because of her. She used to tell me, "Young girls ain't gonna be able to do nothing for you." Looking back in hindsight, I can see now that there were plenty of good women who were directly affected by what my aunt did to me.

It was during that time I made the decision to go find love. What was happening to me at my grandmother's house was not love. It was abuse, and I was tired of being the object of abuse. I called my father and told him that I could not take it anymore and I wanted to live with him. I did not tell him about the molestations, but I told him about the other forms of abuse at the hands of my grandmother. What I heard next made me feel like I was on top of the world. Finally, I would be somewhere, with someone who wanted me. Finally, I would be with someone who loved me. My father told me to pack my bags and come live with him. I could not believe it. Ever since my mother died, I had been waiting for this moment. Now that moment was here. I ran nonstop from the phone booth to the house, only to be met at the door with chastisement for forgetting to do a chore. In those days, my grandmother would punish us by making us write a sentence repeatedly. Whatever we did, we had to write a sentence 500 to 1000 times, stating we would never do it again. For example, if I forgot to make my bed, I would have to write, "I, John Gray, will remember to make my bed in the morning."

After so much writing, your hands will cramp up like crazy! Now, I know why this is corporal punishment in schools. But back then, it was the norm. I don't remember the exact thing I did (it could have been any number of things, knowing me), but I remember writing at the table with my brother Larry. Right in the middle of writing a sentence, I put the pencil down and said, "I can't do this anymore." I told my brother I was leaving and going to live with my father. My brother told me he loved me and I went to tell my grandmother. I expected a long conversation, but all I got was, "Okay then, get the hell out and go live with him." I was stunned. Despite all of the gruffness my grandmother displayed, I did not think she would let her thirteen-year-old grandson just leave the house. I should not have been surprised, but I was. Indeed, she wasn't attempting to stop me, and she added one more thing. I could not take any of her luggage. I was put on a bus to Penn Station in Newark, New Jersey with two plastic garbage bags. I didn't care. I was on my way to live with my father, and everything was going to be alright. No more verbal abuse, no more beatings, no more Aunt Debbie, and no more feeling dirty.

If you recall, I stated earlier that the idealized is better than the realized. I found this statement to be true in the most hurtful way possible. Nothing could ever prepare me for what would happen next. I could barely contain my excitement as the bus pulled into Penn Station. I had spoken to my father the day before and told him what time the bus would get there. I couldn't wait to see him and begin my new life. I started thinking about what life would be like living with someone who loved and wanted me. I started thinking about starting over at a new school, and hoping the teachers would be nicer than my old ones were. My heart started being faster when the bus driver shouted, "Newark Penn Station!" I got up fast, because I wanted to be the first one off the bus. I grabbed my bags and got off, waiting to see my father. I looked and looked, but I did not see him. I waited and waited but no dad. Finally, after what seemed like forever, I went to a phone booth and called him. He picked up the phone and I, excitedly, said, "Dad I'm here. I'm in Penn station. I'm here." What he said next still sends waves of hurt through me. He, very flatly, said, "I don't know why you're here. I can't do a thing for you." Then, he hung up the phone. I was a thirteen-year-old with all my belongings in two garbage bags in downtown Newark. I felt like my heart stopped. I could barely think. I kept hearing his words over and over in my head. I did not know what to do. I couldn't even catch a taxi to his house because I didn't have any money!

I only knew two phone numbers in Newark: his and my Aunt Mattie's. I, also, only knew one other address, and that was 425, South Sixth Street, which was my aunt's address. Despite finding myself in this situation, there were two things I could not and would not do. I wasn't going to call my grandmother, and I wasn't going to cry. I could not and would not do either. I called my Aunt Mattie and told her what happened. After cursing my father, she told me to get in a cab and tell the driver she would pay when I got to her house. As I got into the cab, I still could not believe what had just happened. My shock turned to hurt and my hurt turned to rage. All I was left with were questions. Why did he leave me there? Why did he hang up on me? Why did he tell me to come in the first place? Why didn't he love me? Why didn't he want me?

Hayward House

In my mind, I was back where I belonged, but not how I thought I would. I was born in Newark and spent the first part of my life here, until my mother got sick. I used to come back to Newark every summer after my mother died, because my family, mainly my father, was there. My aunts, uncles, and first cousins were there and I always felt a connection to the city that introduced me to the world. Even as I lived with my grandmother, I longed for the day my father would end my misery and bring me home. I missed my old neighborhood. I missed Chadwick Avenue. I missed hanging with my cousins on 6th Ave. Yes, I was home now, but this was not the homecoming I dreamed about. This was a nightmare, and it was just beginning.

The first thing my aunt did was call my grandmother. I could not hear the conversation because my head was ringing and spinning. I felt like I was on an episode of the Twilight Zone. Aunt Mattie got off the phone and said, "Well you burned that bridge. Your grandmother said no way in hell you coming back there." I didn't say it, but inside I was screaming, "Good, because I don't ever want to go back." As far as I was concerned, I was done living there. What I didn't realize was that I was now homeless. My aunt was my grandfather's older sister, which made her my father's aunt and my great aunt. She was getting up in age and lived alone. The last thing she had on her to-do list was raising a teenage boy. She had been a domestic most of her life and was retired. She did not have much but took pride in what she did have. She always worked on cross word puzzles because she said they helped her vocabulary. She always said that we might live in a ghetto, but we didn't have to act like it. She felt sorry for me, and she called my father. He refused to come to the phone. I knew this because my aunt yelled, "The damn coward didn't even come to the damn phone!" When I heard that, my level of hurt went to a new low. After everything I had gone through, up to that point, I did not think it could ever get worse. But it did, and it was getting worse with each passing minute.

My aunt called my other grandmother, my father's mother, and after a lot of yelling and cursing, sat me down and made things clear to me. According to my aunt, my father didn't even remember telling me come to Newark, because he was high on drugs at the time. He didn't even have a place of his own because he lived with his mother! My aunt ended by saying, "How's he gonna to take care of you when he can't even take care of his own damn self?" Talk about shattered illusions. Once again, I had my spirit broken by a parent; one unintentionally and the other intentionally. My hurt, resentment, and anger finally came to the surface. I cried.

My aunt agreed to let me stay with her, but she had to call DYFS, which is now known as DCP&P. They came out shortly after getting the call and this was when I met my caseworker Mrs. Evans. She would come to play a part in another of my defining moments, but I will speak more about her later. The state signed off for my aunt's custody, but little did I know it would not last long. My aunt spent many days badmouthing my father, and after a while, I got numb to it. In fact, I found myself secretly defending him and his actions. I would say to myself, "That wasn't really him." I held onto a bit of hope that once he got himself together he would include me in his life.

My aunt tried her best, but it is hard for an elderly woman to raise a growing, young man by herself. Especially in the inner city and with very limited resources. I give her all the credit in the world. She opened her home to me, but my wounds were so deep that my psyche was drastically impacted. The loss of my mother. Being torn apart from my siblings. The emotional and physical abuse at the hands of my grandmother. The molestation by my aunt. The rejection from my father. The ridicule from my teachers. It was too much, and I had a perpetual chip on my shoulder. I always had an attitude. No matter how much my aunt tried to steer me in the right direction, I always

22

found a way to rebel and go in the opposite direction. I kept myself guarded and would not let anybody get close to me. I figured that the best way not to get hurt to avoid being close to anyone. I had no relationship with anyone that rose above a surface level. How could I? Up to that point, people had either left me, abandoned me, abused me, or belittled me. I made up my mind that I would live according to my terms, and handle people at an emotional distance. They would never get to know me. I would not give them the chance to hurt me.

My decision to live a guarded life did not make me a happy person. I walked around in a state of anger and depression. I replaced how I really felt with false bravado. If I appeared to be somebody who did not want to be messed with, then I would not be messed with. This attitude did not sit well with my aunt. She told me, on more than one occasion; that if I kept up with my bad attitude, I would be dead in a gutter by the time I turned sixteen. She literally said that to me! I heard her words, and it reminded me of all the other slights I heard in my life. What I have learned to appreciate about my aunt in later years is that, she was trying to give me sound advice. She was only trying to tell me these things for my own good, but I wasn't having any of it. It seemed like I only heard what I had been hearing most of my young life: What I was not, how bad I was, how I would turn out to be nothing, etc. I remember when I turned sixteen. I called her and very smugly said, "I just wanted you to know that I am not dead in a gutter. I'm still here." It was only after I had matured that I realized how arrogant I was to even pick up the phone and say that to her. But this was where I was, emotionally and psychologically. Instead of heeding to her words, I ignored her, and ended up dealing with situations I had no business getting into.

One such situation occurred on Easter in the year 1984. My aunt used to warn me constantly about hanging out with the wrong people and the importance of making good choices. At that point in my life, I thought I knew everything, and she was just being old-fashioned. She approved of some of my friends, especially my friend Reesie, but she did not care for the others. Of my other friends, one who she did not particularly like was Tom, we called him TomTom. She never said why, but she told me, time and time again, that I should stop hanging around with him. TomTom was a little older than I was, so hanging around him made me feel grown up. Given all that I had been through,

23

I thought I was grown already. So, why not hang around with other grown people? My aunt hated it when I said to her, "I am going out to hang around with my friends on Magnolia Ave." I learned why, the hard way.

I remember I was in church, all day, that Easter. I'm talking Sunday School, Sunday Service, dinner after the first service, a second service, and another meal after that one. I was literally in church from nine in the morning until six that evening. As usual, as soon as I got home, I went to "go hang out." While I was with my friends, I saw TomTom's mother talking to people and crying. I wondered what was wrong. She was asking people if they had seen her son. I did see him not long after I got out of church, but it was only for a brief moment. She came up to me, crying, and asked me if I had seen him. I told her yes, and asked her why she was crying. She said the cops were trying to blame him for something he did not do, and they needed to know that somebody saw him that night. I should have taken the hint from Reesie who said nothing, but I said, "Yeah, I saw him tonight. You can tell them I just saw him." What I did not know, until the detectives came to my door, was that TomTom had been arrested for murdering a cab driver earlier that day. Meanwhile, his mother went to the police and told them that he could not have done it because John Gray was with him at the time they said he did it! According to the police, the cab driver was killed around 2pm. I told them I was in church at that time, but it was too late. They already had information from his mother that I had admitted to seeing him around that time. I was taken downtown to the police station to make a statement. My aunt had to come with me, because I was a minor, and she was not happy! She cursed me out all the way to the police station and on the way back. Fortunately, my aunt was in church with me all day. The police took my statement, but they told my aunt they would have to interview members of the church to verify my testimony. The next Sunday, two detectives showed up at First Bethel Baptist Church in Newark. They interviewed everybody from the pastor to the ushers. If I had not been where I said I was, who knows how much trouble I would have been in. It would be easier to think this incident would have made me learn to listen to my aunt's advice going forward. However, as emotionally scarred as I was, even this was not enough.

Not only did my aunt constantly tell me who I should and should not be around, she would also tell me where I should not go. My rebelliousness knew no bounds. It had been instilled in me directly from my traumatic early childhood and teen years. I had every intention of listening to no one, because deep in my heart I trusted no one. I thought I knew best, and I made many decisions that showed me otherwise. I remember my aunt telling me to stop hanging out at the projects, because they were dangerous. Telling a child not to do something was as good as telling them to go right ahead and do it. I thought I was fine because my friend Reesie knew a few people in Prince Street and Stella Wright projects, so I didn't listen to her.

One day, she gave me some money to go downtown and buy myself some clothes for the upcoming school year. She told me to catch a cab back home because she didn't want me walking around with shopping bags of new clothes. This was when that "trying to be tough" exterior came out. I was offended. I thought to myself, "She must think I'm soft! Now she sounds like my grandmother. That is something my grandmother would say." I decided to make a manhood statement. Not only would I not catch a cab back home, I was going to take a shortcut right through the projects! Me and my friend Reesie did just that.

Anybody from Newark can rattle off some of the worst projects in the city in the mid-1980's: McCarter Highway, Hayes Home, Baxter Terrace, Stella Wright, Prince Street, Dayton Street, etc. We put on all our bravado and walked through the projects waving and talking to people we knew. I felt like I was that dude! I said to my friend, "Ain't nobody gonna mess with us. We good." We were almost away from the area of the projects when I noticed these two grown men coming across the street towards us. I didn't think anything of it until a car pulled up next to us and stopped. Before I knew it, I had a gun pointed right at my eye. I froze and couldn't move. All I heard was, "Give me the bags and give me the money!" They took our bags and went through our pockets. I didn't keep money in my pockets, but I did have some in my sock. Then one of them said, "You better come off some money, or you getting a bullet right in your eye." I told him the money was in my sock, and he took the money I had on me. All I could think of, or say, was, "God please, don't let him pull that trigger. I don't want to die." All I saw was the barrel of that gun. I prayed that gun would not go off. They took the money, jumped in the car, and sped away.

Reesie and I ran and tried to put some distance between the incident and us. We got tired after and started walking. Then we noticed the same car speeding up towards us. The car ran up on the curb and cut us off. I thought they were going to shoot us because we saw their faces. We started to run, but one of the men said, "Hey, young boy. Take your stuff back." They were giving us our stuff back! We stood there dumbfounded. The man just said, "Our bad" and they drove away. We didn't know why they did it, but we were just glad we didn't get shot. Later on, I found out that they went back to the projects bragging about the two young boys they just robbed.

What they didn't know was my uncle Lenny was in one of the apartments upstairs calling me from an open window, but I did not hear him. He came downstairs about the same time they were talking about robbing us. My uncle had a lot of respect in the streets, and apparently made the guys find us to return our stuff. The one thing I did not want to do was tell my aunt what happened, because I knew all I would hear from her was, "A hard head makes a soft ass."

That was the first time I had a gun pointed at me. Before I would leave the city of Newark for good, I would have a gun pointed at me two more times. One other time occurred at my friend Reesie's house. We were hanging out when he told me he found his grandfather's rifle in the attic. He showed it to me. It looked old and had a lot of dust on it. He started cleaning the dust off. We both knew for sure that it was not loaded. And it looked old, so we figured that it had not been fired for years. After he cleaned it, he started clowning around, pointing the gun at me. He pointed it right at my stomach. The rifle was literally inches away from me. I laughingly said, "Yo, stop playing man." I slapped the rifle away, and the gun went off! We both froze. We looked at each other, and then, we looked at the wall next to me. On the side of the room where we were, there was a small hole in the wall. We went into the other room and we were both shocked at what we saw. The hole on the other side of the wall was huge! All I could think about was the fact that the hole I saw could have been in my back! Many years later, when Reesie and I reconnected on Facebook, he sent me a picture of that same rifle mounted on his wall. The message he sent me was, "Glad I didn't shoot you bro!"

The other incident was with a police officer. On this day, I was walking down Sixth Avenue, on my way to my Aunt Betty's house, I noticed a lot of cops arresting a bunch of black men. I stopped and looked. Then, one of the police officers pointed a gun at my face and said, "Keep fucking moving!" He didn't have to tell me twice! I told my aunt what happened and she went on a long tirade about how I was eventually going to get in serious trouble one day. As usual, I ignored her words and continued to live as I thought I should. By my own set of rules.

The constant rebelliousness put a strain on my relationship with my aunt. I ramped up the attitude the more I heard her talk badly about my father. In a sense, I was pushing myself out of her door, hoping that things would turn around for my father, and that he would finally come and ask me to live with him. I should have been more careful about what I wished for.

Things appeared to get better for my father. He got married and moved into a place of his own. When I heard he was married, I felt a twinge of resentment. He couldn't even invite me. I felt left out and isolated again. It made me feel even worse to hear that his new wife had a son, and he was taking care of him, while not doing a thing for me. As God is my witness, I cannot recall a moment in my youth where my father gave me a single thing. So why did I want his validation so badly? I wish I had the answer to that. I simply knew I desperately wanted his affirmation. I remember back in the day, when adults used to send little kids to the store to get their cigarettes. My father used to smoke the brand KOOL. In my mind, I thought it was because he was so cool. He was the epitome of early 1970's cool. If you were to watch one of those old Blaxploitation films and see how the pimps dressed, you would be looking at how my father dressed. He was so smooth. His street name was Sweet Thang! I can't make this stuff up! When he used to walk around the neighborhood, all you would hear from the ladies was, "Hey Sweet Thang!" As a side note, I could always tell when my aunt was highly upset with me. She called me by my full name, using my father's last name in place of my own. She would also call me "Son of Thang," very condescendingly. Whenever I heard her say those things, I already knew I was in trouble.

27

I guess, like most children, I had an overly idealized perspective of my father. When you are that young, your father is placed on the hero mantle. So, despite the many times my feelings and spirit were crushed, I longed for any semblance of a relationship. As my father seemingly got his life together, he attempted to reconnect with me, despite the many warnings from my aunt. I thought at the time she was trying to keep me from my father, because, like my grandmother, she did not like him. However, I have grown to realize she was only trying to protect me. In retrospect, I should have listened.

When I was fifteen, my father said that he was sorry about Penn Station. He said that since he was now married, and had his own place, he wanted to make things right. He said he wanted me to live with him, his new wife, and her son. They were living in East Orange at the time. When I told my aunt what he said, she lost it. She screamed, "How can you be so stupid after what he did to you?" The more she talked, the more I became stubborn. I told her I wanted to live with him, and like my grandmother, she told me to go right ahead. I called my father, and this time, he came. I was on my way to live the life I dreamed about as an eight, nine, ten-year-old. I was getting my wish.

Over the course of my life I had heard the phrase, "Be careful what you wish for, because you just might get it." I learned the very hard way that this statement is true. My father picked me up and we drove to a large house in East Orange on University Place. I was so happy to see that my father has such a large place! To me, it felt like validation. I was so proud of my dad, until we got inside. My heart sank. My father was living in a rooming house! I was devastated. I could not believe I left my aunt's house for this. I sat on the steps of the rooming house while my father negotiated a price with the owner of the house. In an odd sort of way, it felt good to see my father going to bat for me so hard. He was fighting for me, and I felt as good as I had ever felt about my relationship with him. Don't get me wrong. I was upset and disappointed to be living in a rooming house. I was not thrilled to be living so close to a bunch of people I did not know. At least, I was with my father, so I rationalized it. I enrolled at East Orange High School and tried to act normal. For a while, things did feel normal. I did have some difficulty transitioning into the new school, because East Orange kids did not like kids from Newark. I did what I always do. I put on my bravado, and gave off the vibe that I was not to be messed with. Fortunately, I made some friends quickly, and had no altercations. For a while, things actually felt good. Little did I know it would get worse. Much worse.

I knew my father drank a lot. Whenever he got drunk, I stayed in my room, and kept out of his way. He was one of those people who would saying anything when they got drunk. I learned to ignore most of it and forgive the rest. However, everyone has a limit. A point where they cannot take it anymore. One day, I reached that point. One night my father got very drunk, and as usual became belligerent. He started banging on my door until I could no longer ignore him. He started yelling at me saying I had to pull my own weight and pay for my own room. This was not the first time I heard him say this, but this time was different. He was drunk and angry. I finally let my anger at him come to the surface. I told him how I felt about everything. How he left me, how he did not come for me, how he never cared. I even told him he didn't even have the decency to come to my mother's funeral. Then he did the unforgivable. Ever since my mother passed, the one thing I could not allow was for anyone to say anything untoward about my mother. In my world of hurt and pain, that was the line in the sand. I cannot count the number of schoolyard fights I got in because of somebody's momma joke aimed at me. That was my limit and my father just passed it. When I mentioned my mother's funeral, he started escalating. He said to me "your mother was a bitch, and I wasn't going to her damn funeral!"

Before I could gather a thought, I threw a punch. I never in my wildest dreams thought I would fight my own father, but here we were fighting, like two grown men in a bar. This incident was the culmination of years of pent up anger, hurt, and resentment. I left the rooming house that night and never stayed with my father again. It was on that night that my realized finally outweighed my idealized. I called my aunt and asked if I could come back and she said yes. After having to listen to my aunt call me all kinds of stupid all night long, we called DYFS again, and spoke to Mrs. Evans, yet again. She had some really bad news for us. She told my aunt that the state was not going to give her any more money. Because I left her house unauthorized the first time, they removed my benefits. Once again, my poor decision placed me in a bad position. My aunt was not having it. She told them that she would give them one week to change their minds or they would have to come and take me. The state did not budge, so my aunt told me to pack my things. She called Mrs. Evans, and once again, a car with the "sun" on the side of the door came and took me away. It was December 20, 1984, and I would spend Christmas in a boys' shelter.

Hayward House no longer exists. I have tried to look it up, but found nothing. Hayward House was a shelter for boys in the foster care system. Since I had no other relatives to take me in, I was processed as a resident of this particular shelter in East Orange. Hayward House allowed me day passes for three reasons: schoolwork, employment, or church. You had to sign out and sign in upon return. The curfew was 8 PM unless you had to work. While I was there, I decided to make the best of a bad situation. I poured myself into school and any activity I could find. In addition, I went to church on Sundays. I became one of the "house leaders," because the counselors said I had a lot of maturity and was not a troublemaker.

I often think about the other boys that were there. We all felt like we were thrown away and that nobody cared about us. I wonder what became of them. I hope they were able to navigate life and succeed despite where we were. I also think of the one counselor whose name I remember, Mr. Mohammed. I remember him because he really cared. We talked a lot, and he used to tell me I had a different spirit. He would often say, "You will be okay." Although I felt far from okay, I found hope in his words, because I could tell he was sincere. I remember that I did not sleep the first night. Most of us boys tried acting tough because we didn't want to be viewed as weak in front of one another. Still, I heard a lot of crying that night. A lot of that tough exterior was a mask to hide fear, hurt, anger, and pain. I placed that mask on as well. It was a defense mechanism I had grown accustomed to. I found it necessary after years of hurt, pain, and neglect. But that night, as I lay in that bed unable to sleep, I could hear many of those same boys, who looked so tough on the outside, crying like babies at night.

I remember a certain day the shelter took us to East Rutherford, where the New Jersey Nets (now known as the Brooklyn Nets) played. The Nets invited some less-fortunate kids to visit one of their practices and gave us lunch. I was not, and am still not, a Nets fan, but I am a fan of one of their players; Buck Williams. The new generation of fans might not know him, but he was an All-Star forward at the time. What I remember most is that, the other players basically ignored us. Albert king didn't even look in our direction. Mike Gminski waved and kept walking. But Buck Williams took time to talk to us. He looked me right in the eyes and told me I could be anything I wanted to be if I worked hard enough for it. Once again, I chose to believe him because I felt his sincerity. There's so much power in authenticity. I just wish more people realized this. I doubt if Buck Williams knew how much he affected me that day. He had probably given that same speech to hundreds of kids, hundreds of times. I don't know how many of them took the time to listen, but I did, and I will never forget his inspiration.

I spent three months in Hayward House. I was fortunate. Most sixteen-year-olds do not find foster families to take them in. Typically, a family wanted a younger child who they felt was less of a risk to upset the balance within their homes. They wanted the cute babies, not growing young boys, especially black inner city boys. At seventeen, most boys got transferred to the youth house in Newark and got lost in the system. I was blessed to have a family that took an interest in my wellbeing. I am forever grateful to the Davis family, who would become my new foster family. They lived on Renner Avenue in the Weequahic section of Newark. They came to know me through a mutual church family. They had no children, and were very hesitant about bringing a sixteen-year-old into their home. I was given a weekend pass from Hayward House for a "trial run" of sorts at their house. The visit went well, and they agreed to start the process of becoming my foster parents. What helped the process work was that I had an aunt who lived in that same part of town. She assured the Davis family that she would assist in any way she could. By now, it was March, and I was going to be transitioning once again. I was excited to be leaving the shelter. To be truthful, I was sick of living with fifteen other boys. With each boy coming into the shelter bringing their own baggage, hurt, and anger, things got testy and chaotic at times.

I saw a lot of fights, and had to defend myself on many occasions. For all of the physical altercations I had been in, I was not a fight starter. I remember something my mother used to tell her kids, "Don't go starting a fight, but if somebody starts one with you, you better finish it." I was tired of the constant collective feeling of hopelessness and despair. In my opinion, if you stay in that state too long, you will begin to think that it is normal. But, I always knew that it was not normal. I had tasted family life before. And even though we were the epitome of poverty, it was still family. So, I always held out hope that there was something better out there. I knew in my heart that there had to be something better than this. I embraced the impending day of my departure from Hayward House. Despite being there for three months, I never made myself comfortable. I never embraced the misery and finality of never being a part of a family. With each passing day, the odds became slimmer that I would ever find a new home. In six and a half months, I would have been on my way to the Newark Youth House and we all heard the stories. We knew that to go there meant going to a black hole. There were no happy stories coming out of the Youth House. It was a pipeline to jail, drugs, death, etc. I will be completely transparent here. I was afraid to go to the Youth House. I wanted more from life and I knew that if I only had an opportunity, I could keep on the road to the promise I made my mother to be good. In my mind, the Youth House was an emotional and social death sentence. And I was not ready to die.

Looking back, I will never forget the look on the faces of the other boys when I left Hayward house for good. What I saw was hopelessness. A part of me was jumping up and down for joy at the thought of leaving. Another part of me was sad that I was the recipient of this opportunity and that I was leaving them behind. I often ponder the following questions: What would I have become if the Davis family did not take a chance on me? What would have happened to me if I ended up at the youth house in Newark? How much different would my life had been? These are simply reflection questions and I thank God every day that I do not have to answer them.

Weequahic

A person's school journey is the most formative experience they will have. Think about it. For twelve or more years, where do children spend majority of their time? For good and sometimes bad, schools influence character, judgment, social circles, and career trajectory. It can be argued that schools have replaced the home and houses of worship as the greatest influencer of youth. This was most certainly true in my case. In the early part of my book, I discussed my troubles fitting in at school. I was bright, but I was always very guarded based on past experiences. Moving in with the Davis family meant going to my third high school in a single year. West Side High, East Orange High, and now Weequahic High School. I was getting used to not making attachments and waiting for the inevitable day when I would be in the main office filling out transfer papers. Given what I had been through, I chose not to be too optimistic, because optimism can be painful.

I enrolled in Weequahic High, which is in the south section of Newark. The Weequahic section of Newark used to be primarily Jewish, but at that time, it was an African American community. I started there in March, 1985 with limited expectations. If I expected nothing, then I would not have to deal with the hurt of unmet expectations. As it turned out, the experience I encountered at Weequahic was very important in shaping the course of my life. I found out that I fit in pretty easily. It probably didn't hurt that I looked just like a boy named Troy who transferred to another school a week before I got there. It turned out that he was very popular. Whenever I walked in the hallway, people would say, "Troy, when did you come back?" I remember one of my classmates, her name was Colleen

Warren, who would always stare at me. She finally told me that I looked just like this boy named Troy who was there not too long ago. The other students soon realized I was not Troy, but it did make my introduction to the school a lot smoother. So wherever you are Troy, thank you.

As you can tell from the preceding chapters, I was and am still huge on sincerity and authenticity. At Weequahic High, I met some of the sincerest and authentic educators. It was refreshing to finally be in the presence of teachers who were not looking to demean you, but lift you up. I met people like Mr. Charles Stewart, who was an English teacher. I don't know how he did it, but he managed to make Shakespeare interesting! Mr. Stewart is responsible for introducing me to one of, I believe, the greatest Shakespeare quotes ever. It comes from King Lear; "Heavy lies the head that wears the crown, and numbered are his days."

Mr. Stewart also happened to be the original minister of music in the hit Broadway play, *Mama I Want to Sing*. The way he carried himself, and the expectations he had for us, was admirable. He set a high bar for us. He was the first black man I had as a content teacher. What I mean is that normally, the black men were gym teachers or industrial arts teachers. His presence was intimidating, yet assuring. He was always immaculately dressed, and he would correct you in a heartbeat if you misused the English language. He did not like slang at all! We all knew that once we stepped foot in his class, we had to abide by his standards. I also had a science teacher named Mrs. Martha Nolley who was also very demanding, yet caring. She was a no-nonsense person, and had high expectations for us as well. To her, it did not matter that we were inner city kids. She expected our best, regardless. She brought that motherly aspect to teaching that I had sorely missed and craved.

I also met a man who would literally change the direction of my life. Mr. Harold Friedman was my guidance counselor. He happened to be a wonderful person, and cared very much about his students. I bring up Mr. Friedman because, I am indebted to him for his kindness and sincerity. Like most kids, I was not sure what I would do after high school. Sure, I was a bright student with potential, but sometimes label stick. Because teachers put me down so early on, I lacked confidence in myself. Even though I managed to keep decent grades through all of my difficulties, I still heard somewhere in the back of my head, the words, "you are a stupid little boy." I was one of a handful of Newark students to obtain a perfect score on my 11th grade proficiency tests, but I was still unsure of myself. I did not consider college because I did not consider myself college material. I thought college was for rich people, smart people, and white people. In my family tree, no one had ever gone to college, and we only had a handful who graduated from high school. I had no one to show me what a college student looked like, therefore, I could not see myself becoming a college student. So, I did what many others had done before me. I enlisted in the military.

One of my good friends at that time, Gerald, came up with an idea. He suggested we go to the Marine Corps together. I wasn't thinking about college, and I knew that as a ward of the court I would have to have a plan in place by my 18th birthday. So I agreed. Because I was a minor, my foster parents had to sign for me. They thought it was a great idea too. However, there was one person who did not like the idea at all. That person was Mr. Friedman. I remember bouncing into his office that next Monday to tell him what I did. I had been sworn-in and everything. I was all set to be shipped off to Paris Island, South Carolina after graduation. Needless to say, Mr. Friedman was not happy. He did not say much, but I could tell he was not pleased by my decision. He got up, went to his file cabinet, and took out my folder. He looked through it, and he looked through some more. He asked me for the name of the recruiter and I gave him the name and number. What he did next both stunned me, and changed my life. He calmly introduced himself to the recruiter, and then said these words I will never forget; "This one is going to college."

I was at a loss for words. I had enlisted. I had been sworn in. My foster parents had signed the papers. When I could finally speak, I shared these thoughts with Mr. Friedman. He simply said, "I don't care. You are not going to the Marines. You're going to college." I had not filled out any college applications, but he was insistent that I was college bound. The next day, I was called back into his office and who did I see? The Marine Corps recruiter! He asked me if I wanted to go to college or the Corps. I looked at Mr. Friedman and said, "I want to go to college." The recruiter said he would stop by my house later that night, to have my foster parents sign the form canceling my induction into the Marines. I was unsure and uncertain about this new direction, but it felt so good to have someone believe in me.

I did not know what to expect when the recruiter showed up at my house, but it was worse than I thought. My foster father and foster uncle literally cursed me out. They called me stupid for choosing college over the Marines. There was that word "stupid" again. In retrospect, I understand why they felt that way. My foster family were from North Carolina and did not go past sixth grade. My foster father was functionally illiterate. This does not diminish the kindness they showed to me by taking me in. I am simply stating the background facts as they were. The only one who stood by my decision was my foster mother Florence, who was one of the sweetest people I have ever known. She gave me the good advice to follow my heart and not regret my decisions. To this day, I still try to follow that advice.

The next day, I went to school and told Mr. Friedman that I was no longer obligated to join the Marines. I shared my concern, that I had not applied to any colleges. He took out some applications and handed them to me. I looked them over. Jersey City State College. Trenton State College. Glassboro State College. William Paterson College. I began filling them out when he said, "By the way, there is a college coming this week to talk about their EOF program." I asked which one, and he said, "Stockton State College."

Stockton

Stockton State College, now known as Stockton University, was a college right in the middle of the woods. The EOF recruiter called it the Pine Barrens. I had never heard of the Pine Barrens, neither had I ever heard of Stockton. I had no idea where Pomona, New Jersey was. I went to the auditorium to listen to what they had to say about a program for low-income families. They explained that EOF stood for Educational Opportunity Fund. They said that students would spend the summer on campus, taking classes and learning about campus life. Then, they threw in the disclaimer. We would have to get up every day at 5:30 AM. We would have mandatory exercise drills in the morning and would have to run around some lake named Fred. We would also have to attend mandatory tutoring sessions, and finally, we could not leave the campus. I said to myself, "This sounds like boot camp. I could have gone into the Marines."

I was not, at all, enthusiastic about going to Stockton, until I heard something that stuck with me. The recruiter said that EOF was a family, and that it went far beyond the summer program. She said they would stay with us from registration to graduation. Family. The word stayed with me. I knew once I turned eighteen I would literally be on my own, and the concept of having a family sounded like a blessing. Despite all the boot camp stuff I heard about the program, I decided to apply anyway. I crossed my fingers and waited to see if I would be accepted.

While I waited for response from the schools I applied to, things were beginning to become sour at my foster home. It was very evident that once I graduated school, I would no longer be able to stay there. This was not an assumption on my part. My foster father said this directly to me. I cannot pinpoint the exact moment when things started becoming sour, but in retrospect, I was as much to blame as he was. I did not make things easy, as I was always guarded and waiting for the other shoe to drop. Sometimes, people who have been through so much drama and trauma cannot function without chaos. Some people even manufacture chaos and sabotage their good fortune, because they are not familiar with good fortune. I believe this was the case with me. I wasn't a malicious kid, but I did have a chip on my shoulder, and an attitude that screamed, "You can't tell me nothing!" I was already used to dealing with transitions, so I just tried my best to prepare for what would come next. Up to this point, my young life had been nothing but a series of transitions, changes, drama, and trauma. What was one more change? All I could do was roll with the punches and not lose heart.

I was also ready to leave Newark. The enthusiasm of the homecoming I felt getting off that Greyhound bus when I was thirteen was long gone. So much had happened in so little time that I was ready to see something else. In Newark, all I saw and felt was struggle and depression. Moreover, I felt like I couldn't breathe. I needed to breathe again. I ran to Mr. Friedman's office with a handful of letters. I had been accepted into a few schools and I was ready to make a choice. Glassboro State College, Jersey City State College, Montclair State College, Stockton State College.

Mr. Friedman and I discussed the options, and I told him I wanted to put some distance between Newark and me. That narrowed the choice between the two Southern New Jersey schools: Glassboro and Stockton. Both schools had an EOF program, and were quite far from Newark. I decided to take it a bit further. I asked Mr. Friedman to show me both locations on a New Jersey map. He did, and Stockton was further down the map, closest to the bottom of New Jersey. Based on the school's location on the map, I decided I would go to Stockton.

My decision to get as far away from Newark was validated on my graduation day. Our high school commencement was held at

Essex County College in downtown Newark. Despite all I had been through with my father, including our fight, I still wanted his validation and affirmation. I called him every day leading up to my graduation, asking him to be there. He promised me that he would not miss it. His track record should have told me otherwise, but I chose to believe that this time would be different. I wanted to believe, with all my heart, that he would not let me down, again. I believed him when he said he wanted to make up for his past mistakes. Again, I put my faith and trust in him. I should not have been surprised when I called him from a phone booth, outside of the college auditorium; and he said he was on his way, but had to take care of something first. I knew what that meant. It was an all-too-familiar feeling. I hung up the phone and resolved within myself that if he came, he came; and if he didn't, he didn't. I promised myself, right then and there, that I would never, again, beg him for anything. I would not put myself through that one more time.

As was his norm, my father did not show up for an important moment in my life. I was hurt, but I have come to believe that God has a way of letting you know that you're not alone. When I was walking across the stage to receive my diploma, a woman who was there for someone else sat next to my brother and sister. According to them, the woman spoke in voice loud enough for them to hear, "I know that boy. He looks like Cat's baby." My brother and sister told me that they turned around towards the person, and when she saw them, she said "Oh my God. You are Cat's kids." Apparently, she knew my mother and my family a long time ago. I took that incident as a sign that despite my father not being there for me, my mother would always be watching over me.

I was packed and ready to go to the summer program at Stockton. True to their word, the program treated me like family. One of their counselors, Yuri Daniels, called me to make sure I had a ride to the school. I told him my sister was bringing me, but it felt great to see that they were looking out for me, before I even stepped foot on campus. As I was leaving, my next-door neighbor, Miss Bernice, yelled, "Good luck, but don't come back!" I laughed, but she was not smiling. She said, "I'm serious. Ain't nothing here. Good luck but don't come back." I did not know it at that time, but I would never call Newark home again.

The closer I got to the college, the more nervous I got. We pulled up and there were a bunch of other students checking in. As far as I could tell, most, if not all were with their families. My Sister Rosie, who dropped me off, could not stay long and left almost as soon as I got there. Once again, I was all alone. Surrounded by hundreds of people, yet I was all alone. Again. I found a bench and took in the sights. I found myself envious of the students who had family there with them for such a big day in their lives. I remember two things coming to mind: it was either sink or swim, and I decided to swim. The other thought was, at least, I had a suitcase this time, not plastic bags!

Almost immediately, EOF lived up to its promise of family. Yuri Daniels, the counselor who called to make sure I had a ride to campus, came over and started a conversation with me. He must have seen the look on my face. His kindness made me feel comfortable. Yuri has since passed away, and I had a chance to speak with him before he passed. He was in a hospital when I called him, and he could not talk long. I wish I had a chance to tell him how much he helped me. He was the tangible meaning of the family atmosphere the EOF recruiter had talked about when I met them in my high school auditorium. This would not be the last time Stockton showed me what family was.

The EOF program was a transformational six-week experience. Up to that point, the only other time I had set foot on a college campus was for my high school graduation. This experience made me feel like an upper-level freshmen. I also got the chance to become part of a family of fellow EOFers, with many who came from backgrounds like mine. I'll never forget my first roommates at Stockton: Turk Hinson from Camden, Gary Smith from Carteret, and Randy Holland from Trenton. The introduction of this new brotherhood meant more to me than anyone realized. I remember one humbling incident where we were preparing to go to Great Adventure for a trip. I did not have the best clothes, and the sneakers I had were paint splattered from when I used to help my uncle paint houses. My roommate, Turk, had a large duffel bag of sneakers. I remember him quietly pulling me to the side and telling me to go in his bag to grab a pair sneakers. I was beginning to see the genesis of my new family structure, where people looked out for each other.

Remember those pivotal and defining moments I mentioned earlier in this book? Two of them occurred at Stockton. The first occurred on my 18th birthday. I turned eighteen on October 31, 1986. This was the day I had been dreading. At that time, in New Jersey, when a ward of the court turned eighteen, they were officially on their own. There would be no more support. Up to that point, I was receiving monthly financial assistance from the state. I knew as soon as I turned eighteen, it would be over. I spoke to my caseworker Mrs. Evans, who informed me that I would receive one last payment on my 18th birthday. She then asked me to come up to Newark, to her office, to pick up the final check. I was dumbfounded. I told her I was a college student with no car and no money. How was I going to get up to Newark from the bottom of South Jersey? Reluctantly, she said she would drive down to the campus with it. I asked her to meet me at the upper J wing. A couple of days later, on my 18th birthday, I met Mrs. Evans at the upper J wing. She did not ask how I was doing. She did not talk about my future plans. She simply handed me a check for $332 and said, "Good luck with the rest of your life." She then turned around and walked away. In my head and in my heart, I thought her actions were cold and heartless. I was hurt to my core. I never saw or spoke to her again. I sat there staring at this check, and that isolated and helpless feeling began to creep back in. This was the moment it all dawned on me. I had to make college work, because I had nowhere else to go. I was literally homeless. I didn't even have the state as a backup anymore. Right there, in upper J wing, I broke down crying. I cried because I was tired of being in those uncertain moments with no one to rely on, or help me. After a while, I wiped my face and asked myself, "What do I do now?" The next thing I did was go to the EOF office for advice. At that time, EOF was the closest thing I had to a family who could help me. So, I dried my tears and headed to the EOF office for advice and comfort.

The second defining moment at Stockton was right after my first semester ended. While the other students were looking forward to going home for the holidays, I knew I had to deal with that lone-feeling again. I did not have a home to go to for the holidays. There would be no holiday reunion for me. No Christmas trees or New Year's celebration. While my roommates left to go home, I had to stay on campus. Alone. One of man's greatest fears is isolation. I came to know why. Being alone is a sinking, depressing state of being. I'm not talking about being alone by choice. I'm talking about being alone, because there are no other options. This was a hard and trying time. I wanted, so badly, to be around family. I would have gladly gone back to Newark if I could. But I did not have that choice. It would just be me, a bunch of Ramen Noodle packs, barely enough food, and the Twilight Zone New Year's Marathon. To this day, I never miss that marathon, because it kept me company. From that experience, I learned that despair is temporary, and that I had to be stronger than my temporary adversity. That time alone made me choose between sinking and swimming, and I chose to swim. I was also given my next glimpse of family and hope when I received a visit from one of the counselors in the EOF Office. They had known that I would be staying on campus over the holiday break, so she dropped by to check on me. She gave me some money to catch the bus into town to buy groceries. That was such an unexpected blessing. It made me feel so good to see that, even though I was alone, there was somebody thinking about me, and looking out for me. Once again, Stockton was living up to its family motto.

Stockton was a transformational experience for me. First, because I connected with lifelong friends. Secondly, because I found people who entered my life and helped me navigate through difficult times. One such person would become my sister for life. I met Ariane Hutchins (now Ariane Newman) at freshman registration, waiting in those long lines in I wing gym. I asked to borrow her pencil and we have been friends ever since. I remember when Ariane, who was on the college meal plan, used to sneak food out of N Wing cafeteria for me. I had no meal plan and I had no job. She was my lifeline, because I had no other means to get food. There is a funny story that she and I still laugh about today. She and one of my other friends, Kim Yearwood, were in the cafeteria and they were getting me some food and juice. I was watching from over the railing, looking like a hungry lost puppy. They had just filled the last thermos with juice when the cafeteria lady caught them! She made them drink all the juice they had packed away. I would get no food and no juice, and they had to leave the cafeteria about to burst from drinking so much juice. Moments like these connected me to others. I did not have to feel like the outsider. I did not have to feel like I did not or could not fit in. I could just be another hungry college student getting by with the help of friends.

My Brother Larry had always been my best friend, but coming to Stockton introduced me to my new brothers. As a result of my time at Stockton, I was introduced to a group of brothers who would be my family for life. These brothers were doing great things on campus, and they stood out. Every freshman, whether male or female, looks in awe at the fraternities and sororities, and what they embody. This is especially true in black culture. To attain fraternity or sorority status, means a lot in our community. It means that you are part of something bigger than yourself, and that you have a family wherever you go. Of course, my first attraction to Iota Phi Theta Fraternity Incorporated was the fact that they threw the best parties on campus. I'm not gonna lie, their parties were the best! They were also very popular. During my time of seeking and searching for which fraternity I would like to have been a part of, I met and had time to talk with some of the brothers of Iota. I realized that there was so much more to Iota than the parties. They talked about all of the community service they did. They talked about their leadership roles on campus. What also attracted me to them was that they were the youngest of the fraternities, and were making a name for themselves, not just relying on a past tradition. Their motto stated, "Building a tradition, not resting on one." After speaking to the brothers, I decided that I wanted to be a part of this brotherhood. I began the pledge process and became a brother of the fraternity on November 7, 1987. My line brother, Marion McClary, now Dr. Marion McClary, was a very studious individual and a marine biology major. I was the more social one, and not seen as overly-studious with my academics. Yet, we bonded, and as fate would have it, both of us would earn doctorate degrees. My induction into Iota Phi Theta was transformational for me, because after my mother died, I lost all sense of my family connection.

As I stated earlier in this book, when my mother went to the hospital that last time, I never again, spent a night together with all of my siblings. Now, here I was, in a fraternity with a new brotherhood, and all of the brothers in the frat were now my roommates. We traveled to other schools together, shared each other's food, and sometimes wore each other's clothes. My frat brother Doc was the one who always had a car so we were always on the road to another campus. We shared the little money we had, and made sure we took care of each other. In fact, it was one of my fraternity brothers, Edgar Green, who opened up his home to me in Atlantic City after my sophomore year. At that point, I had no idea where I would go once school ended. Because he and his family opened up their home to me, I was introduced to another set of family, and I was able to get a job in Atlantic City. It is no coincidence that I would become, even to this day, a South Jersey resident with most of my ties and connections to this region. Because of my new family, I was introduced to the area that would be so pivotal to my life's journey.

Stockton was special to me in so many ways, but more importantly, because I was encouraged to believe in myself. I was given the confidence that I belonged. I was surrounded by people who gave me the support system I so badly needed and wanted. I encountered professors who cared, and set high expectations like Mr. Stewart and Mrs. Nolley did at Weequahic High. These professors demanded that we strive for excellence and put our best foot forward. If I can sum up Stockton anecdotally, I will close this chapter with the following example. I had taken a gerontology course with a professor, Dr. Stow, who had a no-nonsense reputation. At the time, I was working the grave shift in Resorts Casino as a waiter. I got off work at seven, caught the bus to get to campus by nine, and had the gerontology class at 9:55 AM. Needless to say, I was exhausted, and on more than one occasion, I fell asleep in class. Dr. Stow finally called me out of class. I just knew I was in for it. Instead of being chewed out, her eyes softened. What she said, and did next, will stay with me for the rest of my life. She looked at me square in the eyes and said, "When John Gray realizes his potential, John Gray is going to be great." She then asked for a hug. A hug? I fully expected to be chastised for my actions. Instead, she spoke affirmation into me and showed me grace and affection. I never fell asleep in her class again, and I will always be grateful to her, because once again, she was the tangible embodiment of the word that the recruiter used back in my high school auditorium. Family.

My time at Stockton was the beginning of transformation from my cocoon of hurt, anger, fear, doubt, and a lack of confidence. I came through those doors of academia lacking confidence, guarded, and unsure of my future. I walked across that graduation stage feeling accomplished and proud of myself. When I hugged President Vera King Farris as I received my diploma, I felt that I made my mother proud.

Teacher Man, Preacher Man

In my humble opinion, being an educator is the best and most important profession in the world. A teacher influences everyone, at some level. A teacher has the unique opportunity to form, mold, and shape an entire generation. They also have the ability to tear down the spirits of young people, if they are not careful with their words and actions. Given my previous encounters with teachers, I never thought I would become a teacher. At Stockton University, I graduated with a degree in criminal justice, and my aspirations were to become a police officer and a lawyer. My first job coming out of college was in a juvenile detention center. I thought this would be a good entry into my eventual career in law enforcement. I could not have been more wrong. The facility I worked in, housed juveniles aged 10-18, who were either waiting to go to court, or waiting to get shipped to the next level of kiddie jail, Jamesburg Youth House.

There was something eerily familiar about this place. It reminded me of Hayward House. The kids who came and went were usually products of broken homes, as I was while in Hayward House. They also had an overwhelming sense of hopelessness, much like I and the kids in Hayward House felt. There is a word in criminal justice jargon called recidivism. This word translates to repeat offender. It made my heart sick to see the same young boys coming in and out of the facility, much like a revolving door. The sad part of this was that, 99.9999 percent of these boys were Black or Hispanic. The facility was located in a county that was predominately white, yet the vast majority of the boys in this cycle of the criminal justice system were minorities. I worked in that facility for three and a half years, and I can count on my one hand, the number of young white boys who were housed there. It appeared that white kids did not get in trouble or commit crimes, but that was not the case. It was simply a matter of disproportionate arresting. Although, I worked in this facility in the early 1990's, this level of marginalization still occurs.

It was around this same time that I began to undergo a spiritual awakening of sorts. I began to develop a deep wave of empathy for humanity as a whole. I had always gone to church in my youth, but I was not always faithful in living out the principles of faith. I was a typical churchgoer, and I secretly harbored an issue with the church. Before my mother died, she used to keep us in church. I'm talking three services on Sundays and three days a week in-between. My mother loved the church, but I never saw any of those same people after she died. In my days of crying out for help, I used to wonder where they were. I secretly put them in the "fake church-people" category. I carried a lot of that same attitude with me throughout college. I remember getting into an argument with one of my good friends who was a Christian. We went back and forth, and I told him that I got more out of listening to KRS-One than I ever could from reading a bible! Yet, here I was, in a transitional process, and my spirituality would play a huge part in my formation.

I speak of this transition, because I began to see my work in the juvenile facility from a new lens. I began to hurt inwardly for those boys. I saw myself in them, and it got harder, and harder, for me to put shackles on them and lock them in rooms. I am not excusing what they did to be placed in the facility. I am not excusing any criminal behavior that might have landed them there. I am simply stating how my heart began to grieve at the state they were in. My tipping point came when I had to get one of the boys ready for court. He was ten years old, and was going to see the judge. He was shackled by the hands and feet while he was being transported, and it hurt me to do that. What he did next hurt even more. The judge, seeing how young he was, thought he could scold him, and scare him into good behavior. The judge began to tell him how long he could put him in jail. The boy looked at the judge right in the eye and said, "I don't give a fuck! I can do jail!" Right then and there, I was done. I could no longer, in good conscience, spend my career in this maddening cycle of incarceration. I wanted to get to them before they got to such a point. I wanted to influence their lives before the hopelessness and callousness kicked in. I felt like I had been put on this earth to help remove shackles, not place them on people. I am not disparaging the career choice of anyone else. There are people who are in this line of work, yet, do not lose one hour of sleep over it. I just knew, deep down, that this job was clashing with the burgeoning awareness of my own self and my spiritual compass.

I recall when I was at Stockton and there was a career fair taking place during my senior year. Out of curiosity, I began to explore the tables that were set up. I found myself at the table of a recruiter for the Newark City Board of Education. He told me that if I wanted a job as a teacher in Newark they would hire me on the spot. This was because they were specifically looking for black men who would be teachers. When I told him I was a graduate of Newark's schools, he said that was even better. I was guaranteed a position. At that time, I had just begun my job at the juvenile correctional facility, and was still aspiring to be a police officer. I thought about my time in Newark, and how painful it was. I also thought back to my time in school and how unsettling that was for me as well. There was no way I was going to be a teacher! I kindly told the recruiter "thank you, but, no thank you." Now, here I was, at a career crossroads. I wanted to reach children before they got to a place of chains and shackles. Because my background was very similar, I had a desire to reach children in areas where the odds were highly stacked against them. I wanted to affect the lives of children whom I shared similar experiences with. I wanted to help them, because I did not want them to grow up feeling helpless and isolated as I did.

I became a teacher in Atlantic City and began my teaching career as a fifth grade teacher. It was surreal to look in the faces of those children and realize that I had the responsibility to teach, guide, and mold them. I could not help but look at them and see me. For all the hype Atlantic City receives as a vacation destination with elaborate casinos and great beaches, there is another part to the story of this city. For all of its great wealth on one side of the street, there is contrasting stark poverty on the other side. My students came to school with hunger, a lack of resources, from single parent homes, and violent neighborhoods. They needed a teacher to believe in them. They needed a teacher to encourage them. They needed a teacher to hold them to a high standard while empathizing with them. They needed me, and I needed them. This was my opportunity to undo a lot of the wrong that was done to me during my educational journey. It is no coincidence that my spiritual journey coincided with my teaching journey. By this time, I was an ordained preacher, serving as a pastor in my first church. I recall a moment in time when I was fifteen, and my pastor called me into his office. He looked at me very seriously, and then, told me that he sensed a "calling" on my life to become a preacher. At that point, in my life, the church was my safe place. Given all of the turmoil and distress I encountered, I felt peace, calm, and acceptance, whenever I was in church. I felt a sense of belonging, but I certainly did not want to be a preacher! As a youngster, I used to listen very carefully to the sermons, and I would actually try to guide them. What I mean is that, I used to say to myself, "Why didn't he include that, or why didn't he take the message in so and so direction." I didn't realize it at the time, but I was actually in some training of sorts. But I did what most fifteen-year-olds would have done if they were told they were seen as preachers; I ran from it as fast and far as I could. Yet here I was, a teacher and a preacher. I had become what I never saw in my family. In my recollection, I was the first to graduate college and the first to become a teacher or a preacher. I must admit, I am jealous of PKs. That would be Preacher's Kids. I say this, because it would have been a lot easier, if I had someone to help me navigate through the journey of the ministry, as well as my educational journey. It is difficult to be what you do not see. Growing up, the only man I ever saw going to work in the morning, and turning the key in the door every night, was my grandfather. I had no other examples. Now, I was entrusted with two huge responsibilities, with no experience or mentorship to draw on. I now believe that God was telling me that my two callings were intertwined into one path.

I took my role as an educator personally. I still do, to this day. In the nineteen years I served in Atlantic City as teacher and an administrator, I never saw what I did as just a job. While my students and co-workers may not have known it, I was on a mission. I was on a mission to correct wrongs. I was on a mission to influence the lives of children. I was on a mission to give hope. Indeed, I still am. I poured myself into teaching, as much as I did with the ministry, because to me, they were one and the same. Before my students would come in the morning, I would touch each of their seats and say a short prayer. Someone once said to me, that my accomplishments, given what I have been through, made me the exception, not the rule. My response was and is still this: How do you know which child is the exception or which child is the rule? Why not treat each child like the exception to the rule? During my nineteen years, I encountered many students who I could call "difficult." But, the one thing I would never take from them is their dignity and their humanity. I would never look a child in the face and verbalize negativity on them. I would never tell them what they could not be; I would be the one to tell them what they could be. I wanted to be for them what I call, "The Tangible Possibility." If you ask most kids what they want to be when they grow up, they would probably tell you they want to be an athlete or an entertainer. I saw it as my responsibility to show them that you could achieve success in life, without becoming a ballplayer or an entertainer. I wanted to show them that no matter what life threw at you, they had a choice, and it was up to them to determine their destiny. Recently, I received an Instagram message from a former student. His name is Malcolm. Malcolm was one of my difficult students. I can say with all honesty that he gave me a run for my money, and he tested my patience on many an occasion. I heard the Instagram notification come on my phone. At first, I did not recognize the person, because by this time, Malcom had to be at least 30 years old. Then, I read the message: "Hey Mr. Gray, the best teacher in the world! I am seeing the things you are doing in the community. Keep doin what you doin." He had seen an article that I was featured in, on the front page of the Atlantic City Press newspaper. Can you imagine how it felt to get that encouragement, to keep doing what I was doing, from one of my students, who was grown, with kids of his own? To top it off, one of my "difficult" ones at that! There was no amount of money that could have paid for that feeling. I have many former students who still keep in touch with me, and I hope they know they have done as much for me, as I have ever done for them.

As I stated earlier, I began my ministry in conjunction with my teaching career. I began as an AME pastor. I believe my calling into the ministry had as much to do with my healing, as anything else. While I was in seminary, I heard the term, "Wounded Healer." My heart perked up, because that was me! I was, and am, that wounded healer. Humanity at its core, are imperfect beings, but we are to live for the greater good. We are to take the lessons of our scars and help someone else along the way. Being in ministry does not mean you are perfect in any way. I can attest to that on so many levels. Nevertheless, we are to be a blessing to others in our imperfection. I often struggled with this dynamic, but I feel that my journey has made me more of an empathetic minister. I can relate to overcoming struggles like everyone else. I always say that, there is no growth in comfort. Aside from the academic universities where I received my degrees, I like to point out, that I also graduated from the University of Adversity. I remember listening to a minister on television one day, he spent a whole hour bragging about what "sins" he does not do. I said to myself, "He's lying." My life has taught me that every person will have to fight through his or her own fair share of adversity.

I vividly recall three incidents that helped me to understand this concept better. The first was my divorce. I became divorced while I was a pastor. In many church circles, that would mean automatic disqualification from ministry. I struggled with this myself. How could I speak to someone about marriage while mine was falling apart? How could I get up in front of a congregation with any sort of authority, while I failed in such a manner? I made the decision to serve and preach from my pain. I would allow my divorce to place me in a position of the wounded healer. The fact that I was a separated, and a soon-to-be divorced pastor, stayed on my mind constantly. It literally sapped the self-esteem from me. I was able to still preach, but as I always tell people, "Don't let the robe fool you." I was a mess, and I was trying to hold it together. I was trying to put up a strong front, but inside, I was full of anxiety and self-doubt. It was during my separation that I was called to be the pastor of my current church, Goodwill Tabernacle Baptist Church in Philadelphia. The church, which had been the home church of my pastor at that time, was closed for over a year. The membership had dwindled to 6 older ladies, and they desperately wanted their church back. My pastor, Dr. James Pollard, asked me to go help them out and just preach for them. I did, and then, he asked me to go and serve as their interim pastor. I told him "no," three times. Part of the reasons I gave him was the condition of the church. The real reason was my condition. Because of my impending divorce, I felt an unworthiness to serve in the capacity of pastor. Then, he said something that stuck with me. He told me, "God did not call you to be perfect. He called you to serve." I decided to accept the mantle of service, but I felt so over my head. The church was in a physical mess, and there was no membership. The sound of my self-doubt began to overtake my senses. It was not until my installation night that I felt a twinge of relief. As I stood in the foyer after service, I doubted myself all over again. A woman walked up to me and introduced herself. She said her name was Lori Smith, and that she used to be a member of the church. She smiled, and said, "I will be coming back." That was the catalyst I needed! I affirmed my resolve and said to myself, "I can do this." It has been eleven years since that moment, and I am still there, serving from a place of imperfection, but serving nevertheless.

I made up my mind that I would not let my past dictate how I would serve and help others. The experiences I encountered would serve as a barometer for how I engaged others. I would not be as dogmatic when presented with any issues being experienced by someone. I would not be as quick to judge, neither would I be hypocritical. I would simply be loving and available. It amazed me how hypocritical the church could be when dealing with another's issues. I got a phone call from a fellow minister while I was in the middle of my divorce. The call was unprompted, so I thought I was receiving a call of encouragement. Things changed very quickly. He said he called me just to say that he personally does not believe in divorce. I promptly told him that I didn't give a damn what he thought, and that he needs to worry about what happens under his own roof. I feel bad about it now, but I also added a few more words of approximately four or five letters. The other incident that occurred, was when I called a seminary to ask them about their program. The man on the other end was more than happy to help me. I was "brother this, and brother that," until he asked me if I was married. When I replied that I was divorced, he quickly told me that the school would not accept applicants who were divorced! I just hung up the phone on him. I got a sick feeling in my stomach, and I began to detest the hypocritical nature of our churches. In a recent poll, professing Christians lead the nation in divorce rates! How can we be so unloving, when apparently something is going very wrong? My personal stance towards those who are dealing with life from a different lens and perspective from my own, is to simply love people where they are. The very thing I longed for and needed in my formative years was the thing I did not have. Love. Who am I not to give that which I craved the most, especially since I claim to be a minister of the gospel of love?

Looking at the improbable journey my life has taken, I have come to understand that in order to understand suffering, there must be suffering. There is a world of difference between sympathy and empathy. Sympathy does not go far enough. Empathy is that trait which allows one to feel another's anguish and act accordingly. I had to cope with hurt, so that I could effectively help those who are hurting. My life has been filled with uncertainty so that I could comfort those who are experiencing the same dynamic. I have experienced loss and trauma, so that I can have the compassion to help another navigate this life that does not always play fair. I had to deal with failure so that I could, one day, tell someone else that failure does not have to be a dead-end street. Had it not been for my faith journey, I would not have found the strength necessary to battle the years of depression I endured because of my childhood traumas. Yes, I am a pastor who deals with depression! We have a tendency to dismiss issues of mental health, especially in the black community. We either stay silent, or say, "Just pray about it." We eventually suffer in isolation because of our inability to communicate our thoughts and feelings to someone.

I functioned in this capacity for years. I stuffed my hurt, resentment, and anger into a deep, dark place. I, then, went about my business of living as best as I could. I carried my grandmother's words with me constantly, the ones where she told me to shut up "that crying." I went years with no healthy mechanism for coping with my deeper issues. Yes, I loved God and I continued to do the best I could, but my issues always lingered. When a person does not have healthy outlets for coping, they will gravitate to unhealthy ones. That is precisely what I did. I did what so many people, who suffered from what clinicians call Adverse Childhood Experiences, do. They try to drown out the noise of the experience and I did that as well. I remember an incident when I was in seminary and one of my floor mates, who was much older than I was, knocked on my door. He had a large box in his hand and handed it to me. He said to me, "As a minister, nobody is going to know what you go through, and they won't care. Here is something you will need to help you get through those days." I opened the box, and it was filled with all kinds of liquor! He said, "Trust me, you will need it." I should have been surprised, but that was not the first time I had been given that advice from a minister. I gladly took the box and bought into the narrative of making the past go away with a drink, or two, or three. What surprised me about this path was I had sworn that, because my father was a heavy drinker, I would never fall into this trap. I did not want to become like him. It is so ironic that we wind up becoming the things we detest the most.

Through the sound advice of my loving wife Angie, I made the decision to speak to someone about my deeper issues. I was tired of hiding behind my faith, as a reason for not getting the help I needed. I resolved that there was no shame in becoming better. I had my childhood snatched away on so many levels. This meant self-esteem and abandonment issues that constantly haunted me. Because of my prior molestation, I had a hard time relating to what a true relationship was. I was tired of carrying this baggage alone! I was exhausted from constantly carrying my past into my present. I wanted to purge myself from the demons that I felt always haunted me. I was fatigued from trying to mask my hurts in a bottle of Jack Daniels. I was weary of seeking temporary remedies that would only put a band aid on the real issues. It was time to face my fears and hurts head on, and I vowed to do just that. I sought out the counseling that was so long overdue. I am proud to say that; now I do not have to depend on any artificial methods to drown out my past hurts.

I learned through my sessions, that forgiveness goes a long way in the healing process. I had to forgive myself, and I had to forgive others. I had to forgive my grandmother, my aunt, the teacher who called me stupid, Mrs. Little, my caseworker. And, as odd as it may seem to some, I had to forgive my mother for leaving me so soon. Moreover, I had to forgive my father.

Redemption Song

One of the greatest days of my life occurred on October 31, 2009. It was not a fantastic day, because it happened to be my birthday. This was the day I married the person who would change my life for the best. I married a woman who loved me, scars and all. I did not have to be perfect. I did not have to be a finished product. I simply had to be the best me I could be and work on it some more. After the incident with my aunt, I did not know how to properly relate and connect in relationships. Add that to my abandonment and trust issues, and I went into every relationship waiting for the eventual shoe to drop. On several occasions, I hurried the process along with my actions. I sabotaged so many relationships, because I did not trust the staying power of people. My history, up this point, had been one of abandonment and rejection. Why would I expect any different? Nine years later, and I am a better person because I said, "I Do," in 2009. I can say with full assurance, that I do not hold a Master's Degree, if not for her. I do not walk across the stage to hear the name Dr. John E. Gray called at my commencement as I receive my doctorate degree if not for her. I was always an intelligent person, but I always held back, due to the ridicule I encountered early in my life. I was that kid in the class who knew the answer, but would not raise their hand, because they didn't want to seem too smart. Even in undergraduate school, I did not put up the type of grades I knew I could. I did what I had to do to make it through. My wife would tell me I was brilliant, but I did not believe her. Somewhere in the back of my head, I kept hearing all of the negativity. The one thing I learned about myself was that, I responded to encouragement and affirmation. There is something about positive reinforcement that brings out the best in me. My wife flooded my life with positivity and encouragement, and I responded. All my life, I felt like I was alone. Even in my previous marriage, I still felt like I was traveling through life's journey alone. I felt misunderstood and unloved. After so many hits and misses, I finally found love after looking for it in so many wrong places. My wife is a huge part of my redemption story, but there was something else that needed to be done. I had to reconcile with my father.

Not only did my wife encourage me to open up and speak to someone about my past; she also championed the repair of my relationship with my father. My relationship with my father was my Achilles heel. Although we kept in touch over the years, I never gave it my all. I would do the obligatory things, but I would not let myself be sucked into the abyss of optimism. When it came to my previous encounters with my father, I learned that optimism hurts. I remember when my daughter was born in 2011. That was my father's first grandchild, but he never saw her. I would send him pictures during the holidays, but I never took her to do the "grandpa" thing. In my mind, I wanted to protect her and prevent her idealized from ever meeting the realized. I had my idealism shattered so many times, and I did not want her to experience that. What I found interesting, and a little sad is that, he never asked to see her. Not for once did he say, "When am I going to see my granddaughter?" Somewhere deep inside, I wanted him to beg to see her. I wanted him to ask and sound like he meant it! What I conclude now is that, he was probably hurt that I did not take the initiative to bring her to Newark to see him.

My wife won me over and I decided to take the plunge and ask him to come to my wedding. I called him and told him I was getting married, and the first thing he said was, "Again?" Then, he laughed and told me he was just messing with me, and that he would be there. Truth be told, I didn't believe he would come. I braced myself for the eventual excuse. I told myself, over and over again, to remember Penn Station. Remember high school graduation. Remember your college graduation. Hell, remember the promise of the bike he was supposed to get you when you were ten years old. I would not get my hopes up too high, and I definitely would not let it spoil my wedding day if he did not show. We were rushing to get ready, because I did not give my wife a lot of time to prepare. Let me explain. Somewhere in the middle of October, my then fiancée asked what I wanted for my birthday. I said I wanted a wife. I know, it sounds corny, but that was my heartfelt response. We rushed to the township municipal building to get a license, and began putting together the finishing touches for the big day. My wife came up with a suggestion that made me pause. She said, "Why don't you let your father sign our marriage license as a witness?" I stayed silent for a long while. I didn't want to verbalize it, but I did not want to make his signature a part of my plans, just to have him not come. I finally gave in, and we decided to have both of our fathers' sign our poster-sized marriage vows certificate as well.

On the wedding day, I was a nervous wreck. Not only due to the normal wedding day jitters, but also because I was worried that my father would not show up. I did not want to jinx the moment, so I decided that I would not call him. I would take him at his word and let fate handle the rest. As the clocked moved quickly towards the beginning of the service, my father still had not shown. All of the feelings I had felt came creeping back in. It was not anger; it was hurtful sadness. I did not have time to dwell on how I was feeling because the wedding was beginning. I took a deep breath, and we went forward with the ceremony. Although I tried not to show it, I kept looking at the door. That nagging feeling would not go away, even on one of the happiest days of my life. As the festivities went on, I got into the celebratory mode. I was enjoying the moment. I would worry about all of my feelings another time. I was going to enjoy my day. Suddenly, the entire day changed for me! As I was speaking to my sister, I saw my father come through the door. He looked sharp, and was smiling from ear to ear. I will never forget what he was wearing. He had on a navy blue suit, light blue shirt, and an orange tie mixed with a little blue. He looked great! My father struggled with addictions and did not always look healthy when I saw him. Oftentimes, I would be so ashamed of his condition, and try to talk to him about taking care of himself. However, on this day, he looked almost unrecognizable. I was so proud of him. Not only did he make it, he looked better than he had in years. I could not contain myself. I rushed over to the door and gave him a big hug. I loudly said to everybody, "The father of the groom is here!" That moment felt like it made up for all the years of disappointment. I will never forget the look on my father's face. I don't know how many proud dad moments he ever got to experience in his life. This was one of those moments for him, and it definitely was for me as well. My father could not stop smiling as he signed the marriage certificate. I then presented him and my father-in-law with the poster-sized marriage vow certificate. He signed it like a proud dad. I soaked up the moment. I enjoyed the love. I basked in the warmth of redemption.

My relationship with my father would change after that day. It would not be perfect, mind you. It would be far from perfect. My father would still fight his demons, but don't we all have demons to fight? I tried to understand him a little better, as I was a grown married man with a family of my own. It was time to stop seeing him through the lens of the child who felt abandoned at Penn Station such a long time ago. It was time to stop seeing him from the perspective of the child who was hurt and disappointed so many times. I wanted to understand him, because I was just like him. It is true that the fruit does not fall far from its tree, and in so many ways, I was my father's son. I came to understand that like me, he was the baby of the family and was spoiled rotten. He was so spoiled that it stunted and impaired his ability to grow as a man. He leaned so much on my grandfather and grandmother that after they died he was lost in the world. Grown and lost. He carried a picture of me in his wallet. I had to be two years old. My father was barely twenty years old when I was born, and when I looked at his young face in the picture, I saw the hopelessness of an urban youth. My father was first generation inner city. My grandparents came to the North from a very rural part of Georgia, and my father became what we used to call, "*two cent city slick*." In the late 60's and early 70's, times were very hard for people in inner cities. It was a different time and era. I was born a year after the Newark Riots of '67, and I cannot imagine how my father felt as a black man living in that climate. I did my best to understand the paradigm from which my father saw and navigated the world. I concluded that he did the best he knew how; the best he was taught. In the process of understanding him, I came to forgive him.

Redemption takes many forms. One such form can be a homecoming. This is what occurred at Stockton; Again. I titled one

57

of the chapters of this book Stockton, because the university was such a formative place for me. It is where I met adversity, hurt, loneliness, and disappointment. It is also where I met camaraderie, companionship, friendship, and brotherhood. Stockton has been the site of several prominent moments in my life. On January 17, 2017, I was blessed to return to Stockton University as the Assistant Dean of Education. Never in my wildest dreams would I have ever imagined that I would come back as Dr. John E. Gray! Each day I walk on campus, I feel a sense of validation. I feel like I kept my promise to my mother. I feel like I validated Dr. Stow's belief in me when she encouraged me. I feel like the confidence the EOF staff had in me, was not in vain. I also get a sense of validation in the fact that my office in the School of Education is located in upper J Wing, where I received my last ward of the court check when I turned eighteen! I pass by the very spot I sat in as an eighteen-year-old, and I feel a great sense of accomplishment and pride.

Stockton has also been the site of one of my most painful moments. As I was on my way to a meeting on campus, I received a call from my Aunt Betty. She is usually calm, but she sounded very worried when she left a message on my voicemail to call her back. I called her back and the news she gave me hit me like a ton of bricks. She told me that my father had a heart attack, that he was in the hospital, and it did not look good. Five months after coming back, in my new capacity on campus, I was now rushing back to Newark. My head was spinning out of control. Heart attack. I kept hearing the words repeatedly. I do not remember the drive to Newark at all. I was in a state of shock. I tried to think in the most positive of terms, but I did not like the sound of my aunt's voice. She sounded scared. One thing about my aunt: She loved her baby brother. When I talked to her, I felt deep down in my heart that this would not turn out well.

I got to University Hospital, the same hospital where I was born. I rushed to the room and my worst fears were confirmed. No one had to explain anything to me. I did not need a doctor to tell me what I felt in my spirit. My father was gone. Technically, he was still alive, kept breathing by the ventilator. The doctor came in and asked to speak with me privately. Legally, I was his next of kin, and I had to sign some forms. They asked if I wanted to sign a Do Not Resuscitate form, and I signed it. They informed me that my father went without oxygen for hours after his heart attack, and he was now brain dead. They had a procedure whereas they had to perform tests to confirm, but the doctor left that meeting by telling me he was sorry for my loss. I could not think. I could hardly breathe. It was hard to digest and process. The first thing I thought about was the fact that I did not let him see his granddaughter. I broke down and cried uncontrollably. After years and years of this merry-go-round of a father/son relationship, my father was gone. As a minister, I have had to console countless others during their times of grief. I know what to say, and I know when to simply be present. When my father died, I was at a complete loss. I searched for the words, but there were none. I left the hospital feeling as if somebody punched me in the stomach. I cried all the way back home.

The next day, I woke up to a call from the hospital. They told me there was no change, and they needed me to come back to the hospital to discuss how to proceed. They said I had to be the one to make the decision to remove him from the breathing machine because he was officially declared brain dead. I did not want this decision on my shoulders. There was too much left to say. There was still repairing of the relationship that had to be done. I needed for him to know how much I loved him and that I forgave him for everything that had ever happened. After letting the words of the doctor sink in, I realized that I would not get a chance to say any last goodbyes. There would be no more conversations. My father was gone.

I drove back to the hospital on May 13, 2017. I called the family to let them know that my father would be taken off the respirator. We gathered around his bed as the nurse removed the respirator. She left the room so that we could say our final goodbyes. I sat by my father and held his hand. I closed my eyes, and prayed. My wife, aunt, and cousins were in the room with me but I could not hear them. My mind kept racing back and forth. I could not believe I was holding my father's hand as he took his last breath! While I was holding his hand, it dawned on me that both of my parents died in a hospital where either I was born, or my first child was born. In such a short period, the years flooded my mind. I felt trapped in the past while dealing with the pain of the present. As I held his hand, I noticed his breathing becoming shallower. Then, he stopped breathing altogether. All I was left with was the sound of the monitor. It was the sound of a prolonged beep. And it was over. On May 13, 2017, I held my father's hand as he departed this life.

Naturally, because I was a pastor, the family immediately thought I would do the eulogy. I was in a state of denial and grief. I told the family I would eulogize my father. As I drove home, I was filled with grief and regrets. All of the "what if" scenarios popped into my head. I was overwhelmed by my hurt, and I wasn't sure about being able to do the eulogy. My aunt told me that my father would have it no other way. I would have to do it. She told me how proud my father was that his son was a pastor and a successful person. She told me how much he loved me, and that he bragged about me all the time. It was at that moment that I wish I could have some of those early years back. I wish I could have changed so many things. I would have said and done many things differently. That is the lesson life teaches, so I tried my best to focus on the preparation for the funeral.

I went to my father's room to find a suit to take to the funeral home. I opened his closet. He had just one suit. It was in a dry cleaning bag. I opened it up, and it was the exact suit he wore to my wedding! The navy blue suit, the light blue shirt, and the orange tie with a little blue in it. In terms of items, I do not have much to remember my father. I do not have many pictures. I do not have any keepsakes. I decided that I needed something close to him to remember him always. I went home, got my favorite blue tie, and traded it with the one he wore at my wedding. I wanted him to be buried with a part of me, and I would be able to wear a part of him. The funeral home did an excellent job with the arrangements. I looked at him and thought, "He looks like he did at the wedding." Mostly, he looked peaceful, just as if we were sleeping. He did not look sad like my mother looked. He looked at peace and that gave me comfort. As I sat there preparing to do the eulogy, I looked at my daughter. That was the only time she saw her grandfather. I prayed that I did not scar her as I was scarred. At that moment, I felt such a wave of remorse, because the least I could have done was to give him one visit with her. As the last song ended before my eulogy, I felt chained to the seat. I wanted to move, but I could not. The grief held me firm to my seat. At that moment, I did not think I could do it. I searched for my wife to make eye contact. I needed strength, and I needed her. Her look assured me, and I was able to get up. If you were to ask me today what I said, I honestly could not tell you. I felt like I was having an outer body experience. I could hear my voice, but it felt surreal. I had things written down, but I could barely read the words. What I do know is that I spoke directly from my heart. No matter what had taken place in our lives, this was my father lying before me and I was his son. This was the person God chose to bring me into this world, and I was the person God chose to be John Barner's son.

One of the first things I did was ask my daughter if she was ok. Her answer surprised me and made me feel better at the same time. She said, "I had a great time!" She had the chance to meet and play with cousins she never met before. She got the chance to meet aunts who hugged her every chance they got, and who would tell her how much she looked like me when I was a baby. I felt better because I saw how resilient kids can be, and I was immediately reminded how resilient I was. Even though I experienced so many things that fractured my spirit, I still hung in there and persevered. I was reminded of all the times I was hurt, heartbroken, lonely, isolated, ridiculed, violated, and abandoned. Yet, here I was, still standing.

I think of my mother and father often. I think about what life would have been like if things were more ideal. I wonder what would be different had I had the opportunity to grow up with both of my parents, or at least, one of them. What if I didn't have to be in foster homes? What if I didn't have to live with a grandmother who couldn't stand the sight of me? What if my aunt didn't molest me? What if I didn't have to live in a shelter with other boys who felt, like me, were thrown away? What if I was not rudely given my last bit of state money and told to get on with my life? What if I did not have to stay on campus by myself through all of Christmas and New Year? What if I didn't have to depend on friends to steal food for me from the cafeteria? What if I didn't get divorced? What if I let my shortcomings stop me from serving others? My answer to each of these questions is this: Without any of those events, I do not become the person I am today. Each trial allowed me to grow. Each adversity allowed me to become stronger. Each trauma allowed me to become more resilient. Each setback made me wiser. I have learned throughout my journey that life is not always fair. We do not always get what we want. We do not get to choose our parents. We cannot dictate the motives of others. We cannot control the intentions of people. We can choose how we live. We can choose to get up after life knocks us down. We can choose to live outside of our familiar norms. We can choose our own paths, regardless of where we come from. No, life does not always play fair, but we do not have to be bound by its unfair rules. We can rewrite the rules of our own journey. Life does not always fight fair, but we have a choice in how we fight back.

Dr. Gray

One day I was watching television and saw a commercial that sparked my interest. It was one of those genealogy commercials. You know, the one where they get a sample of your DNA and tell you, from an ancestral perspective, where you are from. As I watched the commercial, I began to reflect on my lineage. I began to think about my own family tree. For starters, I was the youngest of nine children, and was only the second among us to graduate high school. My brother Larry was the first. I was the first to graduate college. As much as I basked in that achievement, I had no incentive to go further. As I tell people when I speak at conferences and seminars: It is hard to be what you cannot see.

In my mind, the fact that I graduated from college was something initially perceived as unattainable. I began to search through the branches of my family tree. What I found was heartbreaking. There was a staggering absence of accomplishment in my family line. I did a search in the US Census for my family, and it led me to Burke County, Georgia and Newport News, Virginia. My father's family was from Waynesboro, Georgia. My mother's family was from Virginia. As I scanned the records, I came across something very interesting. I was the product of sharecroppers!

The official language of the records used the word "laborer." I did some more digging and found that this word, in the census report, was code for sharecropper. I looked at the 1930 census of my father's grandparents in Georgia. I looked at the names. I saw my aunt Mattie, who was 13 at that time. I saw my grandfather, who was 10. I saw my uncle Ike, who was only 1. I looked at the names of my great grandparents and uncles, and next to their names under occupation was the word "laborer." Right there, it dawned on me that the more I searched, the more I realized the fullness of my own achievements. For my ancestors, a high school graduation was probably not in their realm of possibility. A bachelor's degree was not even remotely possible. I am certain that they could not perceive of a master's degree or a doctorate degree.

As I dug into my history, my mind wandered to my own journey. I thought of my early years in school, where I was labeled and tagged as unreachable. During my formative years, I was ignored educationally, because no one thought I would amount to anything. I began to think about the struggles of making it through Stockton. Not only was I in survival mode academically, but also emotionally, socially, and economically. My only thought was to hang in there and make it through, however I could. The last thing on my mind was furthering my education. I was very content to settle for a bachelor's degree. To me, that was a great accomplishment, especially as I was the first in my family to reach that goal.

After I became a teacher, I began to feel a desire to do more. Yes, I had conquered the first hurdle, and I had obtained a job in the great profession of teaching. Yet, I kept feeling the tug of my purpose nudging me forward. In 2004, I began my journey in the seminary by attending Palmer Seminary in Philadelphia. I actually relocated to Philly and moved on campus as a 35-year-old full-time student. Keep in mind; I was married and commuting from Philadelphia to Atlantic City, everyday, to my job as a 6th grade teacher. As I was continuing my educational preparation for seminary, I also began to feel the push to further my studies in educational administration.

I loved being a teacher, but I wanted to be able to affect change on a school-wide level. I graduated with my first degree in 1992 and I honestly thought I was done with school. Yet, here I was, thirteen years later, doing two master's degrees at the same time! It was difficult, and many days, I wanted to quit. I had to get up at 4:30 in the morning to get ahead of the horrible morning traffic on the Schuylkill Expressway. I Had to make the hour and 45-minute commute to Atlantic City. Then, I had to get to the seminary and be in class by six, three-days-a-week, and sit, for a three-hour class.

I drew on every ounce of strength I had. In 2006, I graduated with my Master's in Education from Grand Canyon University. I was so proud of myself, but in my heart, I knew I wasn't done. I caught the success bug, and I liked how it felt. I decided I wanted to put myself in rare company. I could honestly say that I knew only a handful of black men with a master's degree, and I knew none who held a doctorate. Although I was excited about the challenge, I began to get those old doubts in my head. I began to hear those old voices. I started to question my abilities and ambitions. Wasn't a master's degree good enough? Who else do you know, personally, that has ever got a doctorate? Aren't you stepping way out of your league? On top of all of these questions, I was in a strenuous marriage that was headed right towards divorce. It was not an amicable divorce either. It was hurtful, painful, stressful, and draining.

I was granted my master's degree on December 24, 2006. By February 2007, I was enrolled in the Doctorate of Education program of Walden University. From that point on, I made two declarations to myself. First, I was going to keep pushing towards my purpose, no matter what I was going through. Second, the calendar was going to keep turning over anyway, so I might as well embrace the moment. It took me 14 years from the time I got my first degree to the time I got my second. I refused to let that much time pass again! I would press my foot on the gas pedal of my purpose and make it happen. It didn't matter to me that I was on a journey where no one in my family had ever ventured before. I wanted to be the first! I took it as a personal challenge to change the branches on my family tree. To me, the degree meant validation on so many levels.

As hard as my first two degrees were to obtain, I knew this one would be more difficult. But it didn't matter. No matter how hard it would get, I would see it through. In my mind, quitting was never an option! I wanted to be Dr. Gray so badly. Before my first class, I wrote my name with "Dr." in front of it. I wanted to put the image in my mind, so I would have a target to shoot for. I was ready for a new challenge, and I was not going to be denied, no matter how long it took, or how much I had to go through.

As I stated earlier, I was beginning this new journey at the same time I was dealing with the pain of an impending divorce. I had to process the paradox of striving for success in one area while failing in another. I had to hone my focus constantly because the stress of the divorce made it difficult to concentrate. I was still commuting over three hours to work each day, so needless to say, I was exhausted! I was so thankful that the program was done online. Even though I had to attend mandatory residencies, on site at the University of Minnesota, it was primarily an online program. I can recall when I first started the program, then I would hear the whispers about the validity of online education. Although people would never say it directly to me; I knew there were those who were saying negative things about me, because I chose the online route. It stung in the beginning, but as I labored through early morning commutes, late night commutes, divorce court proceedings, and life in general, I began to care less and less what people thought! I came to the realization that people are going to have something to say regardless of what you do. What I find so ironic is that today, every university, even the Harvard's and Yale's, have online degree offerings. I put my eyes on my purpose and drowned out the noise, something my life's experiences had taught me so well to do.

I knew the journey to Dr. Gray would be difficult, but I had no idea it would be as hard as it was. Because the program was online, discipline was a necessity to do the required work. You literally had to create your own schedule and make the time. With all of the things swirling around in my life, I wish I was able to have had the opportunity to sit in a classroom. To be a part of the camaraderie of a cohort of classmates. This degree pursuit was a lonely endeavor. I made some friends who were in my group, but it was not the same. As we couldn't just sit and chat with each other on a consistent basis. Also, I began to get disheartened when I saw the number of people leave the program. 35 of us started in 2007, and by 2010, the number was down to six. By the time it was all said and done, only two of us graduated. It took me five-and-a-half years to finish, but that did not matter to me. I finished! Despite those exhaustive commutes, the divorce, the long nights, the doubtful thoughts, I finished. I even managed to remarry. Yes, my hands were full, but I became adept at juggling different things at the same time. I kept the promise I made to myself. On October 24, 2012, my degree from Walden University was confirmed. I was now Dr. John E. Gray!

My commencement took place January 2013, in Miami, Florida. I was so overwhelmed, that I could barely speak. The moment was so surreal. I attended a banquet for the graduates the night before the graduation. Once there, I received the greatest news. My dissertation chair, Dr. Charla Kelley, informed me that she had been given the honor of placing my doctoral hood on me during the ceremony. She had held me together during this process. While I was in the program, her husband passed away from cancer. She told me that he made her promise she would get John Gray through the program. I was so touched, and it reinforced my belief that humanity, at its core, is decent and kind.

On graduation day, I stood in the hall of the convention center with the other graduates. The commencement was not just for the doctoral graduates. The ceremony was for all graduates: bachelors, masters, and doctoral graduates. I looked over the room and two things struck me almost immediately. The first was the disparity between the numbers of graduates in each category. There was a large number of graduates in the bachelor's section. The number dropped considerably in the master's section. When I looked at where I was, the doctorate section, the number was so much lower. The other thing I noticed was that, there were so few black men in my section. I counted about five of us, out over 300 graduates. The gravity of this moment hit me like a ton of bricks. I felt such a sense of awe. I didn't want anybody to see me, but I began to cry with tears of joy.

My wife, four children, my father-in-law, and his wife all came to the graduation. As I sat at the ceremony waiting for my name to be called, I realized that there were so many more who had come with me. My mother was there. My father was there. My siblings were there. My aunt Debbie was there. Mr. Friedman, Mr. Stewart, and Mrs. Nolley from Weequahic were there. Dr. Stow, the EOF program, my fraternity brothers, and my close friends from Stockton were there. My caseworker, Mrs. Evans, was there. The teacher who called me a stupid little boy was there. Dr. Kelley's husband was there. My Aunt Mattie was there. Everybody who affected my life, for good or for bad, was there. I do not get to that moment without the seminal moments that placed me there.

When I heard my name called, I felt like I was having an out of body experience. *Dr. John E. Gray.* I walked across the stage, received my hood from Dr. Kelley, shook hands with the president of Walden, and pointed to the sky. I said, "Mom, your baby did it!" That moment felt so good. After everything I had been through, I did it! I did not let life break me. I did not let my battles defeat me. I did not throw in the towel and give up. I did not quit. I faced down some of the worst things life could throw at me, and I made it. I made it for all of my family who did not have the opportunity to embrace their educational or professional dreams. I made it for my family, like my uncle Lenny, who died of an overdose before he had the chance to see that I would make something of myself. I made it for all those who were still trapped by their inability to throw off the chains of generational stressors that prevented them from excelling. I made it to be able to show others the tangible possibilities attainable if they just believe in themselves.

I am still on this journey. I tell people all the time, "I am just getting started." My life has taught me that no goal is impossible to reach, no matter how unreachable it may appear. Keep striving. Keep going. Keep growing. Just don't quit. On the road to your purpose, quitting is never an option.

ABOUT THE AUTHOR

Dr. John E. Gray is an educator, preacher , motivational speaker and author.
He is the Assistant Dean of Education at Stockton University in Galloway, NJ.
He is also the Senior Pastor of the Goodwill Tabernacle Baptist Church in
Philadelphia, PA. He enjoys reading and spending time with his family. He
uses his voice and pen to inspire others to be the best version of themselves.

Made in the USA
Monee, IL
13 November 2021

81962198R00049